The Discoverers

Cynthia Cochran Kinard

New Harbor Press
RAPID CITY, SD

Copyright © 2025 by Cynthia Cochran Kinard

All rights reserved. No part of this publication may be reproduced, distributed or transmitted in any form or by any means, including photocopying, recording, or other electronic or mechanical methods, without the prior written permission of the publisher, except in the case of brief quotations embodied in critical reviews and certain other noncommercial uses permitted by copyright law. For permission requests, write to the publisher, addressed "Attention: Permissions Coordinator," at the address below.

Kinard/New Harbor Press
1601 Mt. Rushmore Rd, Ste 3288
Rapid City, SD 57701
www.NewHarborPress.com

Publisher's Note: This is a work of fiction. Names, characters, places, and incidents are a product of the author's imagination. Locales and public names are sometimes used for atmospheric purposes. Any resemblance to actual people, living or dead, or to businesses, companies, events, institutions, or locales is completely coincidental.

Ordering Information:
Quantity sales. Special discounts are available on quantity purchases by corporations, associations, and others. For details, contact the "Special Sales Department" at the address above.

The Discoverers / Cynthia Cochran Kinard. -- 1st ed.
ISBN 978-1-63357-461-8

CHAPTER ONE

GRANDPA'S LIPS MOVED, though his prayers were silent. He sat with his head in his hands as he awaited his visitor. His efforts to help his grandchildren seemed to have failed miserably. He had been in this cell for months now with no word of how the children were doing. They had not been discovered yet - that much he knew. But how they were faring, he did not know. All he really could be sure of was that he could trust God and he clung to Him each day with all of the strength that he possessed.

He could not believe it was possible that it had been almost five months since he had left the mountain. For over two weeks after he had arrived here he had avoided detection as he tried to determine just what had happened to his accounts. It was not a simple matter of withdrawing the funds to pay his brother, Charlie's, back taxes, as he had hoped. He had realized that pretty quickly.

He had also uncovered that Sean, his adopted son, had somehow been able to access his funds and his accounts were almost empty. Not that he was a wealthy man. No, that was not it, but he had enough to live on in retirement and that appeared to be almost completely gone. His hope was that the monies had simply been transferred to another account. He still had not been able to determine that, however. In a matter of weeks, Charlie's property would be auctioned off. Not seeing a way to stop that now through his own efforts, his only recourse seemed to be simply to wait and see just how God was going to work all of this out.

"Kevin?"

A woman's voice broke through his reverie and Grandpa raised his head to gaze upon an attractive older woman who looked vaguely familiar.

"Kevin McAlister?" The woman queried again.

"Yes, I am Kevin McAlister. What can I do for you?" Grandpa asked graciously as he stood to his feet.

"I don't know if you remember me or not," the woman began hesitantly, "but I am Nattie Roberts - Caleb Robert's wife - from Stekoah."

"Caleb Roberts? Yes, I do remember Caleb and now I remember you! Where are my manners?" Grandpa asked as he leaned forward with obvious interest in his eyes. "Please have a seat."

"Thank you Kevin," Nattie took the proffered chair, but glanced around to indicate to Kevin that they should be careful with what they said.

Grandpa did not miss her subtle message and quivered inside as he anticipated news from the area where his grandchildren were hidden.

Nattie looked him full in the eyes before she continued. She had to be very careful with what she conveyed. More than Grandpa would be in trouble if she was not.

"I remember you from years ago when you visited our home with your brother," Nattie began cautiously.

"Yes, I remember that visit. Charlie and I certainly enjoyed your warm hospitality. How is Caleb? I have not seen him in years."

At that Nattie dropped her head ever so slightly and said softly, "Caleb passed away a couple of years ago."

"Oh, I am sorry to hear that. He was a good man." Grandpa stated with true compassion in his voice. "I well know the sting of losing a mate."

Nattie's look of empathy came from her heart as she continued, "Caleb was a good man and he thought a great deal of your brother. He would have wanted me to visit you and see if there was anything I could do for you." Once again, Nattie's eyes held Grandpa's with a look that said, please read between the lines.

"I read in the paper what had happened to you and knowing there had to be some mistake, I wanted to offer my services to help in any way I could."

"Mrs. Roberts, that is very generous of you. I certainly find myself in a position where your offer is something of great value to me." Grandpa studied Nattie intently, seeing there a woman he felt he could trust.

"Please call me, Nattie. I feel like we are almost family considering my late husband's close relationship with your brother and how he spoke of you so often and how important family is to you."

"Yes," Grandpa breathed out slowly with deep meaning. "Family is everything to me. My family's well-being has always been at the top of my list."

"And, at the top of mine," Nattie stared deeply into Grandpa's eyes hoping he would catch her double meaning.

What is Nattie trying to say, Grandpa thought. He felt anticipation rising in him, but he tried to conceal his emotions as he glanced quickly at the officer standing nearby.

Nattie smiled her first lovely smile at him trying to help him relax, "Now, there is something I might be able to do to help your family. I understand from the papers that Charlie's property is up for auction for back taxes. Would you know where I could find him so that we could get this resolved?"

Grandpa looked at her intently, "I would love to know where Charlie is myself, but I have had no contact with him in years," Grandpa confessed.

"Hmm," Nattie stated after a pause of reflection. "You have no relatives with whom he might be staying?"

"I have wracked my brain trying to figure out where he might be, but to no avail," Grandpa returned as he took a deep breath.

"Well, it would be a real shame if he lost his land over a matter of back taxes." Nattie continued gripping her purse before her on the table and piercing Grandpa with her dark eyes.

Suddenly, Grandpa realized that Nattie had been wiggling her fingers in a strange fashion and then he caught on. She was using sign language to spell out "children" in a very furtive fashion.

Looking back up quickly as Nattie spoke again, he realized that there was relief in her eyes as she grasped that he had caught on.

"I will visit the courthouse and see if there is anything we can do until we can locate Charlie," Nattie's fingers moved again slowly as she spoke, spelling out "Okay - send love."

Grandpa's relief was palpable but he hurried to speak again lest they be found out, "Nattie, I cannot tell you how much I appreciate your help."

Her fingers moving again as if she was just fingering the strap on her purse, Nattie spelled out "We help them."

"I will let your lawyer know, too, that I will be glad to be a character witness for you. I . . ."

"Time's up, Ma'am," the deputy spoke at her side.

"Take care of yourself, Kevin, and know I am praying for you," Nattie said as she arose from her seat.

"Thank you for all of your help," breathed Grandpa, holding her eyes for a moment and then she was gone, escorted from the room by the deputy.

Grandpa's heart, however, was full of joy. The children were okay. He could breathe again.

CHAPTER TWO

SARAH WATCHED AS Jessie meandered through the cabin, a dreamy look in her eyes. That Jessie was in love was evident to anyone who looked in her direction. Raine's declaration of love could not have come at a better time as far as Sarah was concerned. They could all feel the joy coming from their oldest sister and that took away from the tension of the auction barreling down upon them and their concerns regarding the fate of their grandpa.

Jessie was convinced that Grandpa would eventually be cleared and was happy that she had thought of a way to get a message to him that they were all right. She had taught Raine how to spell her message in Sign Language so that he could teach it to his grandmother. Mrs. Roberts would, in turn, communicate a brief message in this way to Jessie's grandfather.

If all went well, she would see Raine tomorrow and find out how the visit had gone. She could not wait! Not only did she long to see Raine, but she was looking forward to word on her grandpa, at last.

Suddenly Jessie realized that Sarah was rapping on the table for attention. "I'm sorry, Sarah, you were needing me?"

Signing quickly, Sarah grinned, "A penny for your thoughts."

Chuckling, Jessie returned, "Well, today, my thoughts are priceless so you can keep your penny. I am just happy that Raine loves me and that I thought of a way to get a message to Grandpa. I cannot wait to see Raine tomorrow and finally get some news about him."

"And, see Raine tomorrow . . . and see Raine tomorrow . . ." Sarah signed with a big smile enlivening her features.

"I am too readable, apparently!" Jessie laughed as she stretched out on the couch.

Sarah moved to be in the range of Jessie's vision again and then sat on the floor at her feet. "I would be excited, too, if I was going to meet the man I loved tomorrow," she signed with a dreamy look in her eyes.

"Oh, Sarah, one day it will be your turn, too. You'll see."

"I would say that living in seclusion on this mountain has limited my choices considerably," she signed with her silent laughter.

"One day you will venture off the mountain again and God will lead you to the one he has chosen for you and he will be your perfect match."

"I would like that but right now I am very content to be allowed the privilege of taking care of everyone to the extent I do and eventually knowing that we have made it through all of this together as a family unit," Sarah signed.

"You are one in a million, Sarah. You are happiest when you are thinking about everyone else."

Sarah just smiled and arose gracefully to finish her afternoon chores.

Jessie continued to recline on the couch and pray about the situation with Grandpa. He had certainly sacrificed for all of them. He didn't deserve what he was going through. But she knew he would not reveal where they were located for anything in the world. She could not see how this was going to play out, but she knew that the God she served had already been in the future and so He had them all in His very capable hands and had arranged the outcome of this situation, as He had so many others. She could trust Him, this she knew.

She was so relaxed about everything. She just could not be uptight when the God of the Universe loved her and then Raine did, too. How very blessed she was!

Smiling her bliss, she finished her praise to God and arose to help Sarah in any way she could.

CHAPTER THREE

RAINE PACKED THE supplies for Jessie and her family with such gratefulness in his heart that he could help them in this small way. How he longed to do more for them! Securing the saddlebags onto Thunder's back he took a brief moment to give extra attention to his faithful stallion. After all, Thunder had his part in this mission as well. Without him, it would be much more difficult to pull off.

Grandma's shadow fell across the hay covered floor as she stood in the barn door backlit by sunlight. Thunder neighed his welcome as he threw his head up and down in excited greeting.

Turning to survey his grandma, Raine observed her tall, slender figure leaning against the door jamb. He sensed her worry even before his eyes had focused on her features. "Grandma, it will be all right. I will be careful and not take any chances."

"Son, I know you will, but I can't help but be concerned."

"You just keep your prayers going up and I'll try harder to trust God just like I was instructed to do by someone very special to us both," Raine turned his head in that sideways manner of his and smiled his handsome smile.

"Are you coming straight back home?"

"No, I thought I would ride on up and see what I could find out at the General Store. Better to keep the ear to the ground right now, so to speak," Raine finished the last strap and turned to face his grandma once more. "I will be home as soon as I can, though. I can't have my grandma worrying about me."

"Oh, Raine, it's not just you. My heart is threatening to break for the whole situation."

"I know, Grandma, but we are doing all I know to do at the moment. Best leave the rest in God's hands."

Nattie smiled as Raine said these words. Jessie had certainly been a strong influence on her grandson. His young lady possessed a deep faith that could only have come from spending time in God's Word. Nattie could see Raine growing in faith, too. That was certainly worth a great deal and one of the many things for which she had been praying. She was thankful, indeed.

Raine led Thunder out of the barn and reached to give his grandma a quick hug before he left on his trip. She could see the excitement in his eyes as he mounted up and took off down the road. Making her way back to her kitchen she knelt at her table, as was her habit, and began once again to beseech God for the safety of them all.

Making his way up the trail, it was not long before Raine heard voices and knew he was not alone. Sure enough, as he rounded a bend in the trail, he came upon the sheriff and one of his deputies.

"Morning," Raine called out affably in an attempt to cover his nerves.

"Morning, Raine. What brings you out so early or should I even ask?"

Turning his head in that sideways fashion of his, Raine smiled. "Am I that transparent?"

"Well, Raine, everybody knows you are the best sanghunter in this whole county. Figured you must be getting in every moment you can before the season ends."

Raine had already decided to take another sanghunting expedition today to cover his grocery run so he simply replied, "I have a couple more days to get at it and who can blame me when the day is as beautiful as this one?"

"You're certainly right about that," the sheriff replied as he removed his hat and smoothed his wayward hair.

"You fellows taking a pleasure trip this morning?" Raine asked as he eyed the horses which he knew belonged to ole man Crane.

"Well, it is pleasurable being out on such a fine morning, but this is an official business trip."

"Oh?" Raine asked willing his nerves to relax.

"We're still searching for them grandkids of Kevin McAlister's," the sheriff responded as he hit his hat against his thigh to remove the dust.

"Are you thinking they might be in these parts?" Raine ventured.

"To tell you the truth, we don't have a single clue to go on. Only that they are related to ole Charlie. We were up at Castleknob just after daybreak, and looked around all over there. Charlie must have lived in a tent, cause there's no trace of his house anywhere. No sign of footprints or life anywhere, either."

"I've never seen even a trace of Charlie's living quarters and I've certainly been all over this mountain," Raine stated honestly.

Sighing, the sheriff replaced his hat and pulled on the reins, "Well, keep an eye out, will ya'? We'd better be going."

The deputy gave Raine a sideways glance as he rode by that made Raine nervous so he was glad to see them head on back down the trail.

Glancing repeatedly behind him on his way up, Raine made sure he was not being followed. It would not do for the sheriff to suspect anything. He was glad he had only brought part of the supplies. He did not want any humps or lumps giving him away.

Raine was so lost in thought that he arrived at the meeting place before he knew it. He dismounted and looked around to make sure he was alone before Jessie emerged from the kudzu. He longed to take her in his arms, but knew her brother had to be hidden, as well, so with difficulty he restrained himself.

He started unbuckling the straps and withdrawing the packs. Micah emerged, greeting him quietly as he began the transfer. Soon he had removed everything from his person. Micah had stuffed the supplies in his backpack and then was gone as silently as he had appeared.

"Let's take Thunder up to the field and you can go with me sanghunting," Raine began, speaking quietly.

"Do you think it is safe?" Jessie asked, her beautiful eyes round with concern.

Raine just drank in the sight of her and considered telling her about meeting the Sheriff earlier and why he determined it might be safe at the moment. He decided against it, however so just spoke from his heart, "I am beginning to think nothing is safe. We just have to act in faith believing God will protect us."

Jessie smiled at those words. They told her a great deal and she certainly could not argue with their wisdom. "Let's go then."

After leaving Thunder in the field, the two hiked in silence until they were well hidden in the woods. Coming upon a huge boulder, Raine indicated that they sit there and then they could talk.

"I know you are impatient to hear about your grandpa so I will tell you that first," Raine began scouting the area as he uttered the words quietly.

"Yes, how is he?"

"My grandmother said he looked despondent when she first saw him," Raine told the truth gently.

Jessie's heart fell, but she swallowed and looked back into Raine's sympathetic eyes.

"Grandma said he was certainly gracious to her, and did catch on to her attempts at sign language pretty quickly. He was obviously greatly relieved to hear that all of you are fine. He had nothing to offer about Charlie's whereabouts, however. We are on our own there. She believes he was noticeably encouraged by her visit."

"Oh, Raine, I am so thankful she was willing to go. Please convey to her our deepest appreciation. Making that contact means everything to me."

"Jessie, we are trying to think of other ways we can help. If we just had a clue about Charlie's whereabouts . . ."

"I can't help with that any more than Grandpa could. It is certainly a mystery."

"Well, the best we can do is try working out the tax issue ourselves," Raine looked around the surrounding area again. "Jessie, I want you to know we are going to see this through with you. You're not alone in it, okay?"

"Raine, I am just so thankful that God brought you into our lives when He did. What would we do without you and your grandmother right now?"

Smiling, Raine glanced away again. He studied the blue October sky through the tree tops. Soon it would be winter. Would he be able to make it up the mountain if they should have harsh conditions? The past few years the winters had been mild so they were overdue for some colder temps and deeper snows. He had to get this family well stocked up before that time.

"What have you been doing in the winter, Jessie? Have you been able to make it off the mountain as much as you needed to?"

"We stock up during the summer and live off of that when we've had snow or conditions that made traveling difficult. Micah and I have tried to bring in extra staples before winter hits and that has worked so far," Jessie held Raine's eyes with her own as she suddenly realized that she and Micah would not be able to do that this year.

"Well, don't worry. I will try to keep you supplied with extra, as well, and I will stay on top of the weather reports for you. We'll manage somehow," Raine reached over and held Jessie's hand as he looked at her with unveiled sympathy. She certainly had been carrying a heavy load and he was determined to lighten her burden as much as was humanly possible.

"Jessie, I love you and I want to spend time with you. We just have to get this all worked out soon. I want to date you and take you out to dinner and show you off."

Now it was Jessie's turn to look at Raine with sympathy in her eyes. "I love you, too, Raine, and I agree that we need to work things out," she paused and chuckled softly, "I have never been on a real date. Mama and Daddy would not allow it until I turned sixteen and then, of course, we moved here shortly after that."

Raine's eyes lit up with joy, "Then my dear, I will see to it that your first 'real' date is something very special."

Blushing furiously Jessie smiled demurely, "That would be nice."

"Well, let's pray that it will be very soon, too."

Nodding her head, Jessie rose to her feet, "We had best get to work."

"Duty does call, doesn't it," Raine murmured softly as he, too, arose and began the hike into the woods searching the foliage as he went.

CHAPTER FOUR

"WAL, RAINE! WHAT ya' up to today?" Otis called out as Raine entered the General Store. "I've been doing a little sanghunting and enjoying this beautiful day." Raine returned as he deliberately lolled his way into the store.

"Ain't it a purty one though? I's wantin' to git out in it myself a li'l later."

"There are not going to be too many more like this one, so enjoy it while you can, I say."

"Hey, th' sherif wuz by here a li'l earlier an' said he saw ya' up to'ards Castleknob."

Raine stopped in his tracks, "That's right," he finally managed.

"Hope ya got a tow sack full of 'sang' fer me!"

"Well, maybe not that much and when it dries, of course, it might not be much at all," Raine replied, his relief at how the conversation was going not lasting for long.

"Din't see iny of them kids, did ya?" Otis continued.

Not wanting to lie, Raine reasoned that Jessie was definitely not a kid. She was a grown woman now and he had not really looked Micah's way as the teenager had loaded the backpack. After all, he had only had eyes for Jessie. "You mean old Charlie's relatives?"

"Yeah, they's gotta be sumwher's," Otis, much to Raine's relief, was interrupted just then by another customer coming in the door.

After pleasantries and his offer to help the newcomers, Otis turned back to Raine. Seizing the opportunity, however, Raine asked first, "Did the sheriff say if he had found out anything yet?"

"No, he'as buffaloed by it all." Otis rejoined. "T'ain't up on Castleknob, is all he'as figur'd out so far."

Raine was sure that his relief was evident so he turned his head and looked at the customer who was approaching the counter now, "Well, Otis, I had best make my purchases and be going. My grandma will wonder what on earth has happened to me if I don't."

So saying, Raine made his selections quickly and purchasing same headed to the door as more customers were entering. Mounting Thunder, he rode back to the farm.

As Raine was hefting the saddle into its place, his grandma appeared in the barn. "What's the news?" She asked quietly.

"Jessie and Micah met me and were glad to get the supplies. They are well and very thankful to finally have some news of their grandpa. Jessie told me to tell you how much she appreciated what you had done."

"I'm planning to go back and meet with Kevin's lawyer in a few days. His office called me while you were gone and set up an appointment. Hopefully, it will do some good."

"I met the sheriff on the trail as I was heading up."

"You did! Don't tell me they are searching there! What did he say?"

"It went well, Grandma. He had already been to Castleknob and did not find anything. Blessedly, they don't have your ability to smell the tiniest particles of smoke! That early in the morning they just might have smelled some."

"I'm glad he didn't find anything. Was he suspicious about why you were there?"

Raine paused and wiped his shirt sleeve across his brow. "Nothing seemed to be amiss and Otis told me later that the sheriff had stopped by there and said he did not believe the family was up on Castleknob. Hopefully, that will settle things."

Gently grabbing his arm, Nattie breathed out, "I hope so, Raine. Oh, I hope so."

"I must go check on our supper and continue practicing my new 'language'," Nattie smiled. "I'll see you then and we can discuss it a little further," turning she headed for the kitchen door.

Finishing up with Thunder, Raine grabbed his tools and got to work. He had been getting a little behind with his chores and since he was full of energy today he had already decided to get caught up if he could. After all, he had to make this farm profitable. A lot was on the line and he wanted to be in a better position to help Jessie and her family. Making additional monies was certainly one way to assist them. Raine's mind was a whir as he organized his day to get the most possible out of it. He would return tomorrow morning to see Jessie and he wanted to be able to have something to tell her as he delivered the next installment of supplies.

CHAPTER FIVE

GRANDPA WAS SITTING once again awaiting his visitor. He was excited anticipating another visit from Nattie. At least that is the only person he thought it might be. He resumed his praying, interceding as he continually did for his grandchildren.

He glanced up as he heard a woman's footsteps, "Hello, Nattie. Thank you for coming."

"Kevin, it is good to see you again, though I would prefer it to be across my kitchen table," Nattie smiled her beautiful smile as she attempted to raise Grandpa's spirits today.

Smiling, himself, for the first time, Grandpa stood to his feet and indicated the chair across the table from him, "I guess this will have to do at present."

"How are you, Kevin?" Nattie asked as she placed her pocketbook on the table just so, her hands fingering the straps on the backside facing Grandpa.

Glancing quickly at the officer standing a few feet away, Grandpa looked into Nattie's eyes before answering, "I am doing all right. They are feeding me well and I get my exercise. I have a lot of time for praying and that is not bad at all. Of course, like most prisoners, I want my freedom and justice to be done, but I am being treated with civility all in all."

Grandpa looked down at Nattie's fingers as he noticed them moving, spelling out "trying to raise money, must save land, as you well know."

He looked back into Nattie's eyes as she spoke, "I met with your lawyer this morning. He will be in touch with you later about what we discussed, but I hope it will help. It is so ridiculous you being locked up," Nattie finished indignantly. Her fingers moved a little clumsily as she spelled out her next message, "kids well supplied."

Grandpa nodded with gladness, "I find it hard to believe myself, but God knows the truth and that is what matters the most to me."

"Your lawyer is trying to find Charlie," Nattie continued with her eyes fixed firmly upon Grandpa's. "The more character witnesses the better he says and I agree with him."

"I just want to know Charlie is all right. It has been such a long time since I have set eyes on him. Honestly, I am not even sure he is still alive," Grandpa finished with sorrow in his voice.

"Well, we are just going to trust that we can discover where he is, one way or the other," Nattie continued.

"Time's up, ma'am," the officer spoke respectfully.

"Take heart, Kevin," Nattie encouraged as she arose in preparation for being led from the room.

"Thank you, again, Nattie. Please give my best to all those who are praying for me," Grandpa breathed out with sincerity in his voice, hoping she grasped his full meaning.

CHAPTER SIX

"**Y**OUR GRANDPA IS in much improved spirits, my grandma said," Raine shared while holding Jessie's hand as they sat on a fallen log in the woods.

Her smile was worth it all. "Oh, Raine, that is such good news! We will never be able to thank you enough for all you and your grandma are doing for us."

"Consider us thanked. We are only too glad to try to do something while this wrong is hopefully being righted."

He reached over and hugged Jessie close to him. How good she felt and how he did long to set everything right in her world.

Suddenly Jessie's sharpened hearing detected a rustling in the leaves and the next moment a huge buck stepped out into the clearing. He looked in their direction and then turned his head. Jessie, too, turned her head away from him. Raine did the same though he watched the buck out of the corner of his eye. What a beautiful creature and what a huge rack!

The buck walked casually away just as quietly as he had arrived. Jessie looked up into Raine's eyes and saw admiration there. "You never even flinched when you saw the buck or squealed as some girls might have done. It was the same the day those hoodlums attacked you. You just turned and looked at them with quiet courage in your eyes. You impressed me then and I honestly thought you were a young man. How much more impressed I was to discover that you were a female and had faced those boys with such courage."

Jessie blushed as she smiled, "I remember that day and how shocked you looked when my hat fell off."

"Shocked isn't the word. I was purely dumbfounded!" Raine gazed off into the distance remembering the scene and how it had made him feel.

"Seeing your hair spill across your shoulders and down your back was the last thing in the world I was expecting. The sun was glistening off of it and I thought I had never seen anything so beautiful in all of my life," Raine suddenly looked back down at her and continued softly, "I cannot wait until I can see it down all the time. It is a shame to keep such beauty under a hat."

"I wish I could oblige you, Raine, but it is just too dangerous for my family - especially now. Someone just might recognize me from my picture." Jessie replied with sorrow in her eyes.

"Don't worry. I am willing to wait. I, at least, have my memories, after all," Raine replied softly as he turned his head sideways.

"I do have a question about your Uncle Charlie that you might be able to answer. My grandmother said the lawyer was going to try another route to locate him. He will be investigating other places that he might have sold his ginseng besides Otis'. So I was thinking - as you well know sang-hunters occasionally sell their ginseng green, but most likely have been drying some for a while. Have you by chance discovered any 'sang' that your Uncle had drying?"

Jessie replied immediately, "No, and Grandpa mentioned that and how he thought that was a little out of the ordinary. Uncle Charlie must have taken the 'sang' with him when he left. But, he would have sold it to Otis, wouldn't he?"

"Probably, but if Otis wasn't in the store when Charlie left, then he could have taken it elsewhere. There are other buyers in the area, though Otis gives his friends the best deal, I think. I don't believe it would hurt to check around. At least, it is a little something to go on."

"I remember Grandpa did notice that Uncle Charlie either did not have any chickens or had eaten them all or sold them or something because there were no carcasses of any animals of any kind when we moved here. That was something Grandpa mentioned when we thought perhaps Uncle Charlie had possibly died on the mountain in an accident or perhaps naturally," Jessie looked pensive as she tried to remember any other details.

"Hmm, well that warrants another trip to the General Store and maybe I can talk to Pop Caruthers, too. It's worth a shot."

"Well, partner," Jessie began as she rose reluctantly to her feet, "Are we going on another sanghunting run or not?"

"The morning is getting away from us," Raine looked skyward, "but I could stay here with you forever."

Blushing again, Jessie turned her head hoping to cover her reddened face with her hat and headed in the direction of a close patch that she had remembered. Love would have to wait once again.

CHAPTER SEVEN

IT WAS BECOMING more and more difficult to leave Jessie, but Raine reasoned that the more quickly things were resolved, the more quickly he could be with her on a regular basis. So he was headed to the General Store to take the investigation of Charlie's disappearance into his own hands.

Blessedly, the store was empty as Raine entered. Gator, the boy at the counter, indicated that Otis was in his office, so Raine, with determination approached that door.

"Good morning, Otis," Raine called out, with affection for the older man evident in his voice.

"Mornin', Son, wher' ya off to on this fin' day?" Otis asked with a gleam in his eye.

"Been doing a little more 'sanging' so thought I would stop by." Raine hurried on in his impatience, "I've also been thinking about Charlie and what might have become of him."

"Wal, me and Pop heve wandered 'bout thet, ourselves. Ben a topic ov discussion at ire house lately whut wid all thet talk 'bout them kids."

"Do you recall the last time Charlie was in here? Did he have a pouch of 'sang' for you?" Raine knew he was pressing, but he had to know.

Otis raised his eyebrows at Raine's questioning but examined the ceiling as he tried to remember. "Th' las' tim' I seen Charlie, hit wer biz'ness as usual. Now he did cum in here one mor' tim' atter thet but I weren't here. I b'leve Pop talked ta him, but he'd brung sum 'sang' in ta sell an' were dis'pointed thet I weren't here."

Raine's pulse quickened. So he did have 'sang' and probably sold it elsewhere. That could help immensely. "Do you remember anything else?"

"No, Son. Never heerd inythin' bout him atter thet."

"Well, we'll just have to take that and run with it. It is all we have so far."

"Hey, Raine, hev ya seen hide nar har' of thet boy thet used ta cum round here ever week?" Otis eyed Raine as he continued, "Ya know, th' one wid th' purty eyes. I ain't seen him in ah coupla weeks."

Raine felt like a deer in headlights. Surely, Otis could see right through him. His mouth went dry and he swallowed as he tried to think of a response that would not cause him to lie.

Suddenly, Gator stuck his head in the door and told Otis he was needed out front. Raine said a quick good-bye and headed out the door in search of Pop. Saved by the bell, so to speak, he thought.

Pop was in the barn tending to his goats so he was not too difficult to find.

After brief pleasantries, Raine hurried to the point, "Pop, I was just talking to Otis and he indicated that you might have been the last person to talk to Charlie before he disappeared."

After a brief pause Raine continued, "I was just wondering if you recalled that visit and could think of anything that might help me find him."

"Wal now, thet's been sum time back. Ye'd be taxin' my brain to git me to 'member back thet fer," Pop smiled cordially, then chuckled pleasantly.

"You're well known around here for your memory, Pop. Everyone knows that. If anybody wants to know anything they can just come to you," Raine smiled broadly as he voiced this truth to the old man.

Pop ducked his head with obvious pleasure at the compliment, "Wal, I 'member right smart fer an ole feller ifen I do say so myself. Jest why are ya wantin' ta know about Charlie now inyhow?"

Raine leaned against a rough barn pole and inserted a piece of straw between his teeth before he answered.

"As you know, Charlie's property is about to be auctioned off for back taxes and I would surely hate to see that happen. I thought I would see if I could locate him just in the event he doesn't know and maybe we can save his land for him."

"Wal, thet would be the neighborly thing ta do, wouldn't it? I know Charlie would appreciate thet. Anyhows, th' last tim' I seen Charlie wuz the last tim' I believe anyone seen 'im. Least, as fer as I know. He'd cum looking fer Otis ta sell 'im sum 'sang'. He'd also brung two ole hens an' a rooster fer me ta buy. We dickered an' traded around an I got took, as usual. 'Course he let me know that he jest maught be inersted in buying um back frum me when he returned. But, ya know how close-mouthed Charlie was, he wadn't sayin' wher' he'as goin'. He hung tight a li'l more waiting fer Otis ta git back but then said he had ta be on his way. He took off walkin' towerds town an' thet's the last I seen of 'im."

Pop was known to be long-winded so this once, Raine was thankful for that. "If Charlie wasn't able to sell his ginseng to Otis, where else might he have taken it?"

"Wal . . . they's this feller over in Swain County thet pays right smart fer 'sang'. 'Course, no where's as good as Otis. He's th' one ta sell to."

"That's for certain. He buys all of my 'sang' and I've never been unhappy about what he gives me for it. It keeps me coming back," Raine looked across the fence at two little Nubians at play. They were surely cute when they were little.

Not missing a beat, Pop followed his gaze and continued, "Ya in th' market fer sum li'l goats?"

"Oh, no. I've got my hands full as it is with my livestock at the farm. They're just playful creatures, aren't they?"

"Oh, yeah. I'd ruther raise goats then anythin' I can think of," Pops eyes lit up as he talked about his special love, especially since the kids showed cleverness and cunning in the way they played with one another.

"Well, I'd best be going, unless you can remember anything else. Oh, and by the way, do you have the name of the man in Swain County. I'll get in touch with him and see if he might have bought ginseng from Charlie along about that time."

"'Is name's Doc Crisp. Jest give 'im my name. He won't tell ya nuthin' otherwise. Them 'sang' buyers er close-mouthed people ya know."

Raine reached to shake Pop's hand as they took leave of one another, thanking him profusely. Hope was growing in Raine's heart as he remounted Thunder.

Tomorrow he would take the load of supplies up to Jessie and spend the last day of ginseng season with her, then he would be heading to Swain County the following day. As if

Thunder could sense the change in his master's mood, he suddenly took off in a jubilant gallop down the road and Raine relished the feel of his mount under him.

CHAPTER EIGHT

"THIS IS THE last day I can come back up here with a legitimate reason. I am a little leery to travel your way without one. It might raise suspicion," Raine looked deeply into Jessie's eyes as he spoke. He was trying to memorize each facet of her face to carry him through until he could see her again.

"Raine, I do not know exactly what kind of trouble you would be in if it was discovered that you are helping us. It bothers me to put you at risk."

"I'm not concerned about that even though I have a pretty good idea of the kind of trouble. I simply do not want to lead anyone to you or your family. I want you to stay safe," cupping her chin in his big hand, Raine wanted to make sure she understood his reasoning.

"I am working on something right now, but I do not want to tell you about it just in the event it doesn't work out," bending slowly and kissing her gently on the lips, Raine's eyes sparkled in anticipation of being able to tell her some good news at last.

"Well, I will be anxiously awaiting further word," Jessie kissed him back then drew away. "Until then, we had better take advantage of this last day of sanghunting."

Raine reluctantly arose from the huge rock outcropping where they were sitting. They had been careful not to have their conversations in the same place twice. It just seemed to make sense to move around.

Even though they spent most of the daylight hours looking for ginseng, the day with Jessie ended all too soon for Raine. They did find some more 'sang' and that would certainly help towards paying Uncle Charlie's taxes.

Finally, Raine could delay no longer. He was going to be arriving after dark as it was and his grandma would be worried. It was time to take his leave.

"I will be back up as soon as possible with what I hope is good news," Raine began as he pulled Jessie into a hug. "Please take care of yourself until I can return. I will bring more supplies, too. I will think of some reason to come back up just in the event I am stopped."

"Raine, please don't take any chances. We will be fine whether you make it back up or not anytime soon. Of course, I want to see you but not with putting yourself at risk," Jessie's concern showed in her eyes as she looked at him.

"Don't worry, I'll be fine. I just hate to leave you. I want to be with you, Jessie, more than we are. Just know I am doing what I can to work that out. Is your brother lurking somewhere in the kudzu to walk you home?"

Jessie looked ahead to the tangle of vines, "With my being so late he probably is but don't worry if he isn't, I know the way home."

"I'll be glad when I can know it, too, and take you there myself," Raine walked her to the kudzu and then put his foot in the stirrup and pulled himself onto Thunder's big back. He drank Jessie in with his eyes and then headed back down the mountain.

Parting the kudzu, Jessie began pulling herself through. Sure enough she hadn't gone many yards before she sensed

Micah's presence and his flashlight came on to light her way.

"Kinda late, aren't we?" Micah asked in the darkness.

"We found more ginseng patches and ended up with quite a bit. It was certainly a productive day."

"Well, that is good to hear. I just worry about you being out in the woods so much with this man. You're not the only ones looking for ginseng you know. I'm kinda glad the season is over. I know we need the funds for Uncle Charlie, as well as ourselves, but you've really been putting yourself at risk so maybe things can be more relaxed now."

"You don't have to worry about me being in the woods with Raine. He would certainly protect me and besides most people know he works this territory and would leave it alone. I would have, too, if I had known about him, but I am glad it has worked out the way it has. I have felt less anxious being in the woods with him.

Micah pointed his light down the kudzu tunnel before replying, "Honestly, Jess, I think it has been better you going with him, too, but I just wish it could still be Grandpa."

"He'll be back, Micah, I just know it. We'll be together and this will all be behind us soon. In the meantime, God has truly taken care of us. It will work together for good. Just wait and see."

"Well, I certainly admire your faith, Jess." Micah paused and reflected. "You must be hungry after such a long day. Sarah has a terrific stew fixed. She's been keeping it warm for you so eat up when we get there."

"You don't have to tell me that twice! I am starved," Jessie could smell the wonderful aroma before she even reached the door. It was good to be home but she was already missing Raine.

CHAPTER NINE

NATTIE HAD ARISEN extra early as she knew Raine wanted to be on his way to Swain County. Even though she had been helping with his chores he had been falling behind with all the effort he was putting into providing for Jessie and her family. This early start would get him back in order that he would still have daylight hours to work. There was just so much to do on a farm but Raine was well adapted to the work and loved it.

Arriving in their country kitchen, Raine barely had time to wash up as his grandma was already plating up the eggs and bacon. The biscuits sat covered under an attractive blue checked cloth in the bread basket. The home-churned butter graced a round blue antique plate. Raine thought absent-mindedly that he had never known their butter to be put on any other plate since he was a child. He loved these familiar things - they spelled home to him.

"I am ready when you are," Grandma informed as she bowed her head in anticipation of the blessing that Raine would offer.

"Lord, God, our Heavenly Father, we ask your blessings upon this bounty that You have supplied for us. I ask that You would bless my grandma and the work of her hands. Provide safety as I travel today and please bless this trip with success. Keep Jessie and her family safe and work out the issue with Charlie's taxes and their grandpa's situation. Thank You for all of Your blessings but most of all for Your Son, Jesus, in whose Holy Name we pray. Amen."

Looking at Raine with pride evident in her eyes, Grandma passed the homemade grape jelly. "Son, I know you are wanting to get on your way today, so I am going to take care of your chores this morning."

Waiting to swallow the mouthful of bacon and eggs, Raine reached for another biscuit which he buttered liberally, before he spoke, "You sure about that? I can do everything and then leave."

"No, Raine, I want you to be on your way. Who do you think did everything while you were away at school?"

"Aw, that was because you didn't have me here," Raine grinned as he looked her way.

"At any rate, I am doing them today and that's final. I'm anxious for you to get on back here with some good news and the sooner you leave the sooner you'll be back."

"All right. We'll do it your way. I am pretty anxious to be underway myself," Raine swallowed another bite of biscuit and ate the rest of his meal in silence in order to speed things up even more.

Backing the truck up as his grandma stood at the kitchen door with Callie, Raine turned and waved goodbye. He was on his way and it was still dark. His trip should take about an hour so he would definitely be there as this man opened his door. They might have a little privacy that way.

Raine made good time and actually arrived before the business was open. He watched as Doc Crisp made his way to the front from inside the store, unlocking the door and changing his sign to "OPEN".

"Mr. Crisp?" Raine asked as he opened the screen door.

"I am. Ken I help ya'."

Raine extended his hand as Doc Crisp eyed him suspiciously, "My name is Raine Roberts. Pop Caruthers is a friend of mine and told me you might could help me with something."

At mention of Pop's name, Doc Crisp's whole expression changed and his face was suddenly wreathed in a smile which emphasized his twinkling blue eyes. "Wal, come on in, Raine. Any friend of Pop's is a friend of mine."

"Thank you, Mr. Crisp," Raine began but was cut short.

"Let's jest dispense with thet 'Mr.' business. Name's Doc. It's how everbody in these parts knows me. Cup o' coffee?" Doc indicated a pot brewing on the old wood stove.

"Coffee would hit the spot," Raine returned affably.

"Ya known Pop long?"

"It's more like how long Pop has known me. My grandma showed me off to him when I was only about a week old."

"Ya don't say! Wal, you're all right then. How is old Pop doing? Still chasing them goats?"

"Oh, yes. It wouldn't be Pop if he wasn't trying to keep up with his goats. Pop is known far and wide for that." Raine chuckled at memories of all of the escapades he had witnessed through the years with Pop's goats.

Doc laughed so hard at apparent memories, too, that tears ran down the crevices on his wrinkled face. "I tell ya, I've known Pop since we'as both knee-high to a grasshopper and he'as certainly had the adventures. To tell the truth, we'as both had some together. He'as a hoot!"

Slapping his knee, Doc's eyes twinkled with his memories.

"I 'member the time he bought a hog and loaded it up in the back seat of his wife's car," Doc had to stop and laugh before he could continue.

"He rode through town with the hog looking out the back winder and his wife liked to hev killed him when he got home. He got out of the hog business pretty fast after that and went to selling goats."

Raine and Doc laughed some more and made small talk and then Raine thought he had better get to the point before their moment of privacy ended.

"Pop said you might be willing to share some information with me if you had it."

"Wal, what might thet be?"

Raine looked Doc full in the eyes before he continued, "Pop and I both have a mutual friend that no one has seen in about three years. I'm trying to track him down for several reasons. One is that we are all concerned about him and another reason is that his only brother has a real need for his help right now."

"Who is this man?" Doc asked with interest.

"His name is Charlie McAlister."

"Charlie McAlister? Yeah, I know him. Haven't seen him in a few years, though."

"Neither has anyone else, but that is why I came to talk to you. The day he left, he had some ginseng for sale and Pop thought he might have brought it over to you," Raine looked at Doc with anticipation in his eyes.

"Wal, let's see. I remember that day right well. Charlie had hitched a ride into town and had a sack of 'sang' to sell. It was a fine quality and big for these parts. I paid him mor'n I should have hoping to get him back in but I did right well selling it myself. I'd a bought more from him if he had jest come back," Doc studied the old tray ceiling as he spoke, remembering that day.

"Did he say anything about where he might be headed when he left you?" Raine queried hopefully.

"Charlie never was one to share much of anything with me, but he did say he was headed out to take care of some business."

Raine's heart fell as he realized that was probably all of the information he was going to get. Persisting, however, he asked, "You didn't notice what direction he was headed in when he left, did you?"

"No, I don't recollect back thet far," Doc paused and poured another cup of coffee for himself and offered more to Raine, "and, he never really said where he was going."

"Well, Doc I truly thank you for all of your time and the coffee," Raine said, refusing the offer of another cup, "I had best be going. Work is waiting for me back at the farm," Raine stood and shook the hand extended to him. Placing his hat back upon his head he turned and walked away.

Raine had almost attained the door, when Doc hollered out, "Hey, wait a minute. Don't know if this would help or not, but he did mention he had to be on his way. He'as catching a bus some where's."

His eyes alight once again with hope, Raine left Doc's company and driving down the street approached the bus station. Did they keep records dating back that far? Would they share them with him if they did?

Parking his truck, Raine took a deep breath as he approached the station. It was an ole timey station as were so many businesses in this town. There were a couple of people obviously awaiting the arrival of their bus, but the ticket counter had no line. The man on the other side of the counter was an old timer such as Doc and that in itself gave Raine fresh hope.

"Ken I he'p ya?" The man asked cordially.

"I am certainly hoping so," Raine began, "I don't know if it is possible that you keep records from some time back, but I am looking for someone who took a bus from here about three years ago according to Doc Crisp. It was he who told me you might be able to help me."

"Say Doc sent you. Wal he and I go way back. He'as a good man. What ya be needing?"

"Well, about three years ago a man by the name of Charlie McAlister took a bus from here and I was hoping to find out where he might have been going," Raine stated, his heart in his throat.

"Charlie McAlister, Charlie McAlister . . ." the ticket agent rubbed his stubbly, wrinkled chin as he thought back obviously trying to remember.

"He'as a friend of Doc's, weren't he?" The agent looked at Raine as he tried to recall details.

"Yes, he was a friend of Doc's and also Pop Caruthers, if you know him, from over at Stekoah," Raine watched the agent carefully hoping to trigger his memory.

"Pop Caruthers! Yeah, I know him! How is the old coot? Haven't seen him in a coon's age!" The agent became animated as he recollected Pop.

Raine heard the door close behind him and turned to see someone approaching the counter. He moved respectfully out of the way and waited while the young man bought a ticket. After the agent documented the transaction, Raine resumed his place.

"Just what were you needing to know about Charlie McAlister?" The agent looked back up as he spoke, addressing Raine.

"Charlie has been missing for about three years and I am trying to locate him. He apparently transacted some business with Doc and then came your way to purchase a ticket. We are trying to determine just where he was going when he left here on the bus, if you keep records back that far."

"Oh, we keep records, but having a date would be helpful."

"I really only know the month and year unfortunately," Raine lamented as he heard the door close behind him again.

Two more people came to buy tickets and once again Raine stepped aside and waited patiently.

As the agent finished documenting the second sale he looked back up at Raine, "Maybe it would be best if you would give me your phone number. I'm going to have to research this and it might take some time with handling the counter, too."

Raine gave the month and year of the last sighting of Charlie and then gave his number, instructing the agent to go ahead and give his grandma, Nattie Roberts, the info if she should answer.

"Nattie Roberts! You don't say! Well, I knew yer grandma and Caleb right well. Heerd tell Caleb passed away a few years back. I'as sorry to hear that," shaking his head as he spoke.

"By the way, name's Deal. Give my best to yer Grandma," the agent tucked the slip of paper containing the info into his shirt pocket and looked back up as the door opened once again interrupting their conversation.

"Thanks for your help, Mr. Deal. I look forward to hearing from you," Raine finished quickly as the new customers approached the counter.

He headed back to his truck, glancing around at the quaint little town as he left. Maybe this was the beginning of the end of the search for Uncle Charlie. Raine smiled broadly as he thought it over and headed back to the farm.

CHAPTER TEN

CALLIE RACED TO the truck as Raine drove up. She was jumping with excitement to see her master return. Raine paused long enough to rough-house with her and then headed to the kitchen door.

He could hear his grandma on the phone as he approached. She sounded excited and as he entered the kitchen, he noted that her face was flushed.

"Thank you so much, Mr. Deal, I'll bring a basket of apples for you the next time we come your way for all of your time and effort. No, I'll certainly see that you get them. Yes, he is a fine young man. Well, take care of yourself and we hope to see you soon," Nattie turned to Raine, her face still flushed.

"As you probably heard, that was Mr. Deal and he did indeed find the record of Charlie's bus trip," she paused, her eyes glistening with excitement as she made sure she had Raine's full attention.

"Well?" Raine asked with great anticipation.

"Charlie was headed to Ninety Six, South Carolina," Nattie breathed out with relief.

Raine's eyes reflected his hope as he took this in. Why Charlie had not returned crossed his mind, but he pushed the thought back as he clung to this possibility of discovering him in the near future.

"Would you like to take the day off tomorrow and go with me to Ninety Six?" Raine asked as he looked at his excited grandmother.

"You know, I just might do that. I could get up early and fix us a picnic and we could just enjoy the day, too," anticipation rimming her voice, Nattie looked at her grandson with affection.

"Well, let's plan on it. I will go ahead and get started and work as late as possible today so that I can get a jump on everything tomorrow."

So saying, Raine headed for the door once more to get his work done and as excited as he was it would be undertaken with fresh energy. The mystery of Uncle Charlie could end as early as tomorrow. Raine wanted to leap in the air as he thought about that.

Conversation was still laced with hope for the future as Raine and his grandma enjoyed a late supper. They would head out the next day for Ninety Six and hopefully be able to locate Uncle Charlie. Both outlined their plans for the next morning in order to streamline their chores as much as possible. An early start was what they were aiming for and would work hard to be able to accomplish this.

Sleep did not come easily to Raine, however, as he fell wearily into bed. His thoughts were all a jumble. The new friends he had made that day, Uncle Charlie and his whereabouts, and, of course, Jessie and her grandpa. What a difference finding Uncle Charlie could make to everyone concerned. His excitement could not be contained until weariness finally cast him into a deep and refreshing pool of sleep. He did not awaken until he heard Natalie's rooster crowing the announcement of a bright new dawn. Ah, at last! Maybe this day would bring the answers they sought!

CHAPTER ELEVEN

JESSIE HAD KNOWN this was coming. She and Micah had discussed it. The leaves were falling from the kudzu vines and it would not be long before she would be visible as she crawled through at the end of the tangle of vines. It was possible that by the next time Raine came up the mountain there would be no more leaf covering.

Right now, Raine simply believed that they were hiding in the kudzu until he left. He did not realize that was their way home. Of course, Jessie had not intended to deceive him, but had not contradicted what he believed.

After hashing things out, Micah thought it would be best if Jessie came up with a different place for her to meet Raine. What else could they do?

Jessie thought long and hard about another meeting place and decided that it would be possible to hide herself pretty well amongst the boulders strewn at the edge of the field below Castle Knob. She would just have to be at the boulder near the kudzu vines well before Raine at their next meeting time. As it stood now, Raine knew that he would not be back for several days but she was to begin waiting for him on the fourth day at their usual time. If he showed up she would be there and if not, she would simply have spent that time in prayer. Then she could tell Raine about their new meeting place for the future at a certain boulder below Castle Knob.

Nevertheless, concern nibbled at Jessie. It would only be a matter of days before she could be seen pulling herself through the tangled web of vines. What if someone other than Raine should be nearby? After all, that was still the only way she had of coming and going. They would be in a real mess if someone did see her.

Jessie thought all day and into the next about their dilemma. She really did not want to share this with her family, but it certainly involved all of them whether she wanted it to or not. Oh, why did that boulder have to fall and block the entrance to the cave? They were at greater risk of discovery now than they had ever been.

Finally, the only solution that presented itself to her tired mind was to go and come under cover of darkness. She could leave while it was still dark in order to meet Raine in the mornings but returning would still be in daylight. That just would not work. Therefore, they would have to meet at night. But if they did that Raine would be going down the treacherous trail after dark. Every solution seemed to have its drawbacks.

After their noon meal, Sarah noticed that Jessie seemed unusually fatigued. Gaining her attention, she signed, asking Jessie what was wrong.

"Oh, I just have my mind on some things," she smiled at her sister, "I didn't know it showed, however."

"You just seem unusually tired," Sarah signed, watching Jessie carefully.

"Sarah, you know me too well. As usual, I have been trying to figure something out on my own when I should have been praying about it. It has literally worn me out! But thanks to you, I see where I have been going wrong. I will rest tonight, enjoy the little ones and then get a good night's sleep. Starting tonight I will be praying about this issue as I should have been doing all along. When will I ever learn?" Jessie smiled lovingly at her sister and then stretched luxuriously while she reclined on the couch.

Smiling her own special smile, Sarah left her sister alone and went to check on the children. They had been too quiet. She discovered them in the barn with Micah and Josh watching a new baby goat.

The twins were sticking their heads through the rails and looking at the baby longingly. How they wanted to play with this new addition to their family! Katie, meanwhile had perched precariously on the top rail of the enclosure and little Annie was attempting to climb up to her.

Before Sarah could gain their attention, Micah saw the situation and reached in time to gently grab Annie and place her beside Katie. He held on tight to Annie and Katie grabbed his arm as she almost lost her balance.

"Do you really want to sit up here, Katie, and run the risk of falling into the pen with the baby? Don't you think that would scare it? And, besides, if Annie had crawled up here on her own, she might have fallen off and gotten hurt. You've got to set the example for her, Katie, don't you think?" Micah asked gently.

Sarah could have burst with pride as she heard her brother. He was very much like a father to these little ones and had taken over so much of the responsibility since Grandpa had left. She walked over softly and helped Katie as she climbed down. Micah placed Annie beside her and both little girls stayed put as they drank in the sight of the soft little creature.

Suddenly, Sarah was filled with such love for her family and she knew in her heart that God would somehow keep them all together and if it was on Castleknob for the rest of their lives that would be all right with her, too. She truly loved it here and if Grandpa and her dad could just be with them it would be almost perfect. She breathed in deeply of the smells of hay, goat and sweaty brothers and turning with a full heart and joy in her surroundings, headed back to the kitchen.

CHAPTER TWELVE

THE PICNIC BASKET had been packed, the chores had all been done and Raine and his grandma were finally underway. They were both filled with hope that today they would resolve the mystery of Charlie's disappearance.

The trip should take them about an hour and a half and so they had plenty of time to discuss possibilities and make some more plans for their future on the farm.

"Grandma, how many different types of herbs do you have in your garden now?" Raine asked with interest.

"Oh, law, I transplanted quite a few and, of course, I already had a mess of them so I'd say forty-one or two. The ones I transplanted have done well this year. I didn't lose any. Of course, they'll start spreading out next year," Grandma's eyes had taken on a dreamy look. She truly loved working in her herbs.

"I noticed that some of your patches that you've had for years did particularly well this season," Raine continued.

"Oh, yes. Of course, my mints outdo themselves. The problem there is trying to contain them. Your grandpa buried some flashing around them years ago to keep them from taking over the other plants. The lemon balm and sage did very well this year and we can sell all you want of them next year."

"I have been working on lining up some buyers for next season and I think that will certainly be another income stream for us then. I will prepare some more larger beds enclosed with flashing so that you can transplant some of your mints to other areas and just let them spread as much as they want to," Raine clutched the steering wheel and slowed down as three deer stepped into the headlights in front of his truck.

"Beautiful creatures, aren't they?" Grandma asked as the three leapt up the bank their white tails in the air.

"They are that. I saw some grazing in the upper pasture, but with Callie around I don't think they will be much of a threat to your new gardens, but we'll keep a watch on things just the same," Raine sped up again after checking to make sure all of the deer had indeed crossed the road.

"I was inspecting your largest patch and when I told one of my potential buyers about it he said we probably had several thousand dollars of herbs in that one patch."

"You don't say! Well, I never thought we could raise that kind of money. And that was just for one patch?" Grandma asked incredulously.

"Yes, Ma'am. That's what he said. If I could have gotten a little earlier start with things this year, we could have already made the money. There is just a lot of planning that needs to go into it, harvesting at the prime time and all. Plus, we will need additional help eventually. And, speaking of additional help, I have been checking into raising Christmas trees and would like to plant a few fields of those next year. That will give us a wonderful income stream in future years," Raine's voice was laced with excitement as he spoke and that was not lost on Nattie.

"Sounds like you have been doing a lot of thinking and planning. Your grandpa would be proud," Nattie reached over and laid her hand on Raine's arm as she spoke.

Raine gulped and looked away. Sometimes the subject was still too raw.

"It is lightening up. Glad we were able to leave so early. Just don't know how much time we might really need today," Raine attempted to cover his emotions with the change of subject.

"Well, Raine, I got up early this morning and prayed a while about this situation. I asked God to lead us in the right direction and help us to discover just where Charlie might be. I'm expecting to have some news that we can go on to try to clear this matter up."

Raine looked sideways at his grandma. She never ceased to amaze him. They had to get up earlier than usual as it was. So she arose even earlier to pray about the situation? She was incredible.

"Unfortunately, I did not think along those lines. By the way, while you were praying did you get any leading?" Raine asked hopefully.

"None yet, but don't be surprised if He doesn't either lead us straight to Charlie or at least to someone who knows where he might be," Grandma turned and smiled as she spoke.

Raine chuckled. His grandma had faith. He would give her that.

Suddenly the sun appeared on the horizon and its brilliance was dazzling after the morning's darkness. Both grandma and grandson delighted in the beauty of the display. It was certainly worth getting up early to witness such an event.

Within the hour they saw the sign indicating that their turn to Ninety Six was just up ahead. They would be to their destination well before most offices opened so Raine suggested they stop at a coffee shop and look at a phone book and get their bearings.

The coffee shop was quite busy and they sat patiently awaiting the waitress. They talked about Charlie and where they should begin their search.

"Ya ready to order?" asked their rosy-faced waitress at length.

"Grandma, are you wanting something besides coffee?" Raine asked.

"Actually, I was thinking about one of your homemade cinnamon buns," Grandma stated as she looked up from the menu and smiled at the waitress.

"Will do, and what for you, Hon?" asked the waitress as she smiled appreciatively at Raine.

"Just make that a double with coffee for each of us," Raine returned respectfully.

"Have it out in a minute," the waitress replied as she turned over their cups and poured their coffee.

As she returned with their cinnamon buns, Grandma could see the steam rising from them. "Don't those look good!" She exclaimed.

"They are good. We sell a lot of them. They are our breakfast specialty. Say, you folks aren't from around here, are you?" The waitress asked eyeing Raine.

"No, we're from Stekoah, in North Carolina," Raine replied congenially.

"You just out for the day or thinking of moving down or something?" The waitress pressed, still smiling at Raine.

"Actually, we're here looking for someone," Raine responded.

"Oh, just who are you looking for, maybe I can help," the waitress asked never taking her eyes from Raine.

"Well, maybe you can. We are looking for a gentleman named Charlie McAlister. Ever hear of him?" Raine asked hopefully.

"Charlie McAlister? Hmm . . . sorry I can't say as I have ever heard the name," the waitress suddenly turned to an older man sitting a couple of tables away. "Hey, Henry, you ever hear of someone named Charlie McAlister?"

The man named Henry turned towards them, "What's that? Charlie who?"

"Charlie McAlister," the waitress repeated and looked around as someone hailed her for more coffee.

"Sorry, Hon, I got to get busy, but Henry here knows everyone in these parts," the waitress smiled again sweetly at Raine and left to do her business.

Henry moseyed on over to their table and Raine graciously moved over and offered him a place to sit. "Charlie McAlister? Can't say as if I have heard the name before. Did he just move down?"

"Actually, he left where we live up in Stekoah almost three years ago and no one has seen him since. We know he took a bus to Ninety Six and that is all that anyone knows."

"You don't say! Been gone that long. Well, that's a shame! Relative of yours?" Henry asked with obvious concern.

Nattie spoke up at this point, "He is a neighbor of ours and nobody really knew for certain that he was gone until a short while back. We didn't have any clues to go on until just this week and now we are trying to track him down."

"Say he come here on a bus?"

"Yes, sir," Raine returned respectfully.

"Hmm . . . almost three year ago, you say?" Henry stoked his whiskered chin as he wondered aloud.

"That's what we believe," Nattie replied.

"Well, I don't know of anyone named Charlie McAlister but long about three years ago now, there was an old man who was struck by a vehicle of some sort as he crossed the street. He was hurt pretty bad and in a coma and all for a long time. My wife happened to be in the nursing home at that time when they brung him in. She died about a year ago and so I ain't been back but he was still there the last time I was. No one knew who he was at that time. Don't know if that could be your Charlie McAlister or not, but it might be worth checking out."

"Henry, I am awful sorry to hear about your wife's passing. I certainly know how that feels," Grandma responded sympathetically as she looked at the old gentleman in front of her.

"Oh, it was hard losing her," Henry replied with tears suddenly rising to his eyes, "But, ya know she's better off. It was hard to see her lying there and not getting any better. They's a lot of hard cases out there at that nursing home, even though it is a particularly good one."

"Well, Henry, we will check it out ourselves when we leave here," Nattie stated.

Raine also expressed his sympathy and asked Henry for directions to the nursing home. They talked some more with the old man, who was obviously lonesome and discovered that he took his breakfast every morning at the coffee shop. He had been a regular for some time.

They finally said their goodbyes and thanking the waitress for her part in connecting them with Henry made for the door.

"Ya'll come back anytime now," the waitress called as she winked at Raine, whose face was still flaming as he leapt into the truck.

Grandma chuckled and asked her grandson if he did not realize what an attractive man he was and, of course, he was going to garner his share of attention.

His face flaming again, Raine backed out of the parking lot and headed his truck in the direction of their goal.

CHAPTER THIRTEEN

THE NURSING HOME proved to be only about fifteen minutes away from the coffee shop. Raine and his grandma looked at each other and took a deep breath. This could be it and how they hoped it was.

Raine, as always, held the door for Nattie and she marched with purpose to the desk. After greeting and explaining their mission to the lady on duty, they were instructed that they would have to talk to the administrator who was out on one of the halls. After being paged on the PA system, a pleasant-looking woman in her forties approached and greeted the Roberts and then led them to her office next to the front desk.

Nattie took the proffered chair and sat upright as she began the conversation, introducing herself and Raine and briefly stating that they were looking for someone. "We don't want to keep you long, as with your position you must be a very busy woman."

The administrator nodded her head, but stated, "I am always busy, but our purpose here is to see to the needs of our residents and if we can be of assistance or enhance their stay in some manner, we are always willing to try our best."

"Well, we are not even certain that the man we are looking for has ever darkened your door, but we had a lead this morning and we are simply checking it out," Nattie stated honestly.

"We understand that between two and three years ago, a man was placed in your care who had been involved in an accident where he was struck by a vehicle and was in a coma for some time," Nattie began.

"Oh, yes. We had been caring for this man for some time, not knowing just who he was," the administrator responded with interest.

"You said 'had' been caring. Is he no longer with you?" Nattie asked as she leaned forward and gazed into the woman's eyes, dreading the probable answer.

Reading Nattie's concern, the administrator answered quickly, "Oh, it is not what you might think, the gentleman, we called him 'Gent', was discharged day before yesterday. We were all very happy for him and gave him a little going away party. I wish you had come a couple of days ago," the administrator stated with regret.

"Well, we are happy for this gentleman at least, whoever he was, but did you ever determine his name or did a family member come and get him?" asked Nattie, though her disappointment was mounting in her eyes.

"It was very interesting how it all came to pass," began the administrator as she leaned back in her chair to tell them the story. "We had finally been able to give 'Gent' physical therapy on a regular basis and he had gained strength and it was obvious that he was going to be able to take care of himself again. The only problem was that he did not remember who he was and only had the money he came in with to leave on. We were trying to resolve the situation with the authorities and get him some help, when something happened out of the blue. 'Gent' was taking his daily walk around the halls when he happened to spy a newspaper and it stopped him in his tracks. He grabbed the paper and sat down in a nearby chair as if his legs were just giving out on him. The lady who was walking with him said he looked like he had seen a ghost and turned very pale. She ran and got the nurse and when they returned old 'Gent' looked up at them and said he knew who he was. Splattered across the front page of the newspaper was a bunch of his relatives. Can you imagine?" The administrator smiled at them as she asked the question.

"Charlie McAlister," was all Nattie said.

"Why, yes! That is exactly who he is! So, he must be the man you are seeking?"

Nattie reached over and grabbed Raine's hand with a big smile on her face, "That is, indeed, the man we have been seeking!"

"Oh, my! Then you know his brother is in a passel of trouble," the woman said as she sat back up in her chair.

"He's in trouble all right, but he did not do what he has been accused of. He definitely needs his only brother right now and his brother needs him, too, for other reasons." Nattie looked back at Raine.

"Ma'am, do you know where Charlie might have been heading when he left here?" Raine interjected.

"He didn't say exactly. He just said he knew who he was and things would be all right now. We all took up a collection for him and then returned the items and monies we had found on him when he first came here. Odd thing was, however, there was not one piece of identification on him, no driver's license or anything else."

"Well, Charlie didn't drive so he wouldn't have had a driver's license and having no other identification is certainly not surprising to those of us who know him. We cannot thank you enough for sharing everything with us. It will definitely change a lot of people's lives. And, thanks, too, for taking such good care of Charlie. God just placed him into your hands and you did what was necessary," Tears of joy were streaming down Nattie's face as she spoke. Charlie was alive and now well enough to be on his own!

CHAPTER FOURTEEN

RAINE HELPED HIS grandma into the truck and then walked around to get into the driver's seat. He wanted to run, however, or leap into the air he was so excited that they had found out about Charlie.

The two just sat in the truck a few moments as reality began to sink into their beings. Raine could not wait to report his findings to Jessie. How relieved everyone would be!

He looked at his grandma and realized that tears were still streaming down her face though she wore a huge smile.

"Grandma, are you all right?" Raine asked with concern.

"Oh, Raine, I just knew he was alive but I am filled with awareness that God led us pretty much straight to where he had been living. We need to stop and thank Him!"

"Okay, Grandma, I agree. Do you want to or do you want me to?"

"Would you mind if I did?" Nattie asked as she looked deeply into Raine's eyes.

"No, Grandma. Please go ahead. After all it was you who got up early this morning and prayed for this very thing." Raine looked at his grandma and then reached over and clasped her hand.

"Oh, Father God, we are filled with joy at how you have answered our prayers and led us to the ones who could tell us about Charlie. Thank you for the wonderful care that you provided for him after his accident. Thank you for restoring his memory and I pray your blessings upon this nursing home and those who cared enough to give him a sendoff. I pray for this administrator and for wisdom in all of her dealings. I pray for Henry that You will fill the void in his life and for the waitress who helped us and obviously has been good to Henry. Please provide safety as we continue on our journey today and lead us in the next step in finding Charlie and saving his property. And, Father, thank you for the blessings of Your beautiful sunrise and allowing us to see the deer this morning in time that none of them or us either were hurt by the encounter. We simply were allowed to enjoy them and all of Your Creation today. Help us to do Your Will the remainder of this day and to enjoy Your Presence. It is in the Holy Name of Your Son, Jesus, that we pray. Amen."

Grandma's face was sheer radiance when Raine glanced at her. She was such a special person and Raine uttered a quick prayer of thanks that God had placed him in her care all of those years ago.

"Well, we still don't know where Charlie is, but I believe we will know before too very long. It is enough for me just knowing that he is alive. I do believe, however, that you should pay another visit to the courthouse. Maybe when they hear the circumstances they will give Charlie a little forbearance," Grandma said as she turned to face Raine.

"Maybe we should pay a visit to the bus station here before we leave and find out where he went from here," Raine suggested.

"Let's do that," Grandma agreed.

The visit to the bus station, however, proved fruitless. Charlie had not left town on the bus. Not knowing what else to do, Grandma suggested they find a grocery store on the way home and stock up with some more supplies for Jessie and her family.

On their way back they discovered a picturesque little park and stopped to have their picnic. Once again, Grandma had outdone herself and emptied the basket to reveal a regular feast. They sat and enjoyed the meal and the moment and each other. Some things you just didn't want to rush.

After the meal, Grandma blessed the birds and squirrels with some of the leftovers. They actually came right up to her and would almost eat out of her hand. Raine marvelled anew at his incredible Grandma!

They packed up and continued on their way discussing just where Charlie might be at this moment and how very good it was going to be when they finally saw him. Eventually they came upon the grocery store and in their exuberance bought extras for Jessie's family. Nothing made then feel better than when they were doing for others.

CHAPTER FIFTEEN

GRANDPA SAT ONCE again awaiting his visitor. He was anxious to see Nattie. He was hoping she would sign more news about his grandchildren. How he missed them!

He heard the guard approaching and looked up. Surely his eyes were deceiving him! It couldn't be! But there standing before him, bent and leaning on a cane was none other than his only brother, Charlie!

"Well, aren't you going to say anything or are you just going to sit there gaping like you've seen a ghost?" Charlie asked gruffly.

Grandpa felt himself rising to his feet as if in a dream and reached to hug his brother before he realized that was not allowed. He felt the tears streaming down his face, but he did not care who saw them. His brother was alive and standing right before him! He drank in the sight and then realized just how much Charlie had aged since he had seen him last. The browned, healthy glow he had always had was no longer there. He was gaunt and looked like a man who had suffered long and hard.

"Charlie," Grandpa finally choked out, "I can't believe this is you standing before me!"

"Well, who else would it be when you need so much help?" Charlie asked matter-of-factly.

"Please sit down and tell me where you have been. I have been worried sick about you," Grandpa confessed unashamedly.

"Where I have been is not much to talk about right now. The important thing is that I got out yesterday and came here as quick as I could. I understand we only have a few minutes and we need to be talking about how you got yourself into this mess and how we're going to get you out," Charlie eyed his brother levelly.

"You are willing to help me . . ." Kevin began only to be cut off by Charlie.

"The past is in the past. We don't need to waste time. We need to get you out of here."

"The bail is too high for that," Kevin acquiesced and went straight to the point. "I am here until this thing is settled. You need to talk to my lawyer. He is just down the road on Second Street - Hal Sutton. He can fill you in on all the details."

"Did you do it?" Charlie's gaze was penetrating as he looked at his brother.

"Of course not! I love my grandkids as you well know!"

"Just needed to hear you say that. I am here to help you, Kevin, but you've got to help me help you."

"The best thing you can do right now is forget about me and help yourself. Were you aware that your property is up for auction?" Grandpa asked leaning forward.

"It is? Well, that don't surprise me none as long as I've been gone."

Grandpa gazed intently into Charlie's eyes, "Go see Nattie Roberts. She is trying to save it for you. You also might want to look in Dad's old mantel clock."

"Dad's old clock? How the world . . ." but a look from Kevin stopped Charlie's flow of words and he just gazed at his brother. Dad's old mantel clock was still sitting on his mantel in the cabin the last time he saw it. Was it possible?

Kevin just looked at Charlie knowingly, pleading with his eyes for him to read between the lines.

"Time's up," the guard said as he approached Charlie to see if he needed any help getting up.

"Don't waste any time until you take care of those taxes," Kevin stated emphatically as Charlie arose slowly. Kevin continued with his heart in his words, "and, Charlie, I can't tell you how glad I am that you are back!"

CHAPTER SIXTEEN

THE LEAVES HAD almost all fallen from the vines as Jessie made her way cautiously, stopping every few seconds to peer about and listen to make sure she did not hear anything. It was almost daylight, but nevertheless she knew if anyone saw her that her whole family would be at great risk.

She finally extricated herself from the vines and then hid behind the closest boulder. The morning was downright cold and Jessie was already shivering as she positioned herself to wait. She had always believed that the first cold spell was the hardest to bear.

Rubbing her hands together and blowing on them did little to help as the wait lengthened. Daylight came and Jessie knew it would still be quite a while before Raine made his appearance, if indeed he could come today. She prayed fervently while she waited and repositioned herself numerous times trying to stay warm. They would have to come up with a better plan in the future or else she would need to bring a blanket. Her coat was not a very thick one at that and even though Sarah had insisted on her wearing a sweater underneath, she was still shivering. She had always been moving before when she hiked off the mountain and then back up in the cold so she had never felt the downturn in temperature quite like this before.

Ah! The sound of hoof beats was music to Jessie's ears. In her haste to get up and get moving, she raised her head over the top of the boulder to check out the situation. Immediately she knew that she had made a mistake! This was not Raine. She crouched down again quickly and willed her teeth to quit chattering but she knew in her heart that she had been seen.

"All right, you know I saw you. Come on out!" The man called gruffly from on top of his horse.

Jessie's heart was stuck in her throat. She wanted to run, but where would she run to? All around her was uphill except for the path that the man and his horse was on. She would not get far running with the speed of a horse after her. The only option was to face this peril and so praying her favorite Scripture with great fervency she stood to her feet.

"Come out from behind that boulder where I can see you!" The man moved his horse closer as he yelled.

Jessie, knees knocking, came around the boulder and waited as the man approached on his horse.

"What are you doing up here, young man?" The man asked sternly.

"Out with it and look at me when I speak to you! I want to see your eyes and just who I am dealing with!"

Jessie gulped and then did the man's bidding. Suddenly the man drew backwards upon his horse and then composing himself, leaned down, "Ain't you one of Kevin's grandkids?"

At mention of her grandfather's name, Jessie knew she had been caught. Her identity was exposed. The peril to her family flashed quickly through her mind but she stepped closer and looked the man full in the face. Something looked familiar about him, however. Where had she seen him before? Then suddenly she knew!

"Uncle Charlie? Is that you?" She asked incredulously.

"I am Charlie McAlister, though I'm not used to being called 'Uncle'. Which one are you?"

Jessie wanted to cry out with joy as she suddenly realized the significance of just who was standing before her. "Uncle Charlie! You're alive! We didn't know for sure but we have certainly prayed for you for so long. I can't begin to tell you how very glad I am to see you!" Suddenly Jessie shivered violently from both the cold and a releasing of her fear.

"Child, you'll take your death of cold in that thin coat. Come on, I'll take you to my house and warm you up and you can tell me about what you're doing here," Uncle Charlie said with compassion "and you ain't told me your name yet."

Jessie did not know what to do except reach up for Uncle Charlie's extended hand and hop up behind him as she told him her name. They rode the rest of the way to the table rock and the little stream below Castleknob where she jumped down from the horse and helped her Uncle, who was very stiff and descended with great difficulty.

Uncle Charlie stood there for a few minutes and got his bearings and attempted to walk out his stiffness, Jessie helping. "You said your name is Jessie. Which one are you now in the lineup of things?"

"I'm the oldest," she looked him full in the eye as Uncle Charlie leaned in closer for a better look.

"Well, I'll be. You're the little gal I met up on the rocks that day. I can certainly see now that you are not a young man. Sorry for the mistake," Uncle Charlie stated apologetically.

"No need to apologize. I intentionally look like a young man," Jessie replied.

Uncle Charlie looked at her as the meaning of her words sank in and then smiled broadly, "Something tells me there is more to this story, but we need to get to my cabin and get you warmed up first."

Then he looked up at the little bonsai-looking tree and suddenly saw the boulder that was blocking the cave. "Oh my," was all he said.

Jessie decided to take this opportunity to address her concern, "Uncle Charlie, I know you had some difficulty with my grandpa in the past and all."

"You said it. It is in the past," her uncle said as he gazed down at her. "I saw the news in the paper about you and your siblings and I am here to help your family and Kevin. I just didn't know any of you were up here until a few minutes ago. I was headed to the mantel clock in my cabin to see just what kind of message your grandpa had left me. I figured it was about you kids but I was not expecting to see one of you up here."

"You saw Grandpa? He knows you are alive?" Jessie asked, her eyes shining.

"Yes, he knows and he knows what kind of trouble he is in but all he could think about was me saving my property and you kids. If I can get this boulder removed we can go on to my cabin and warm up and get to the bottom of this," Charlie gazed again at the boulder and rubbed his stubbly chin and headed in that direction.

Suddenly he turned around to make sure she was following and asked, "What were you doing hiding behind that boulder anyway?"

Jessie took a deep breath. "I was waiting for someone."

Looking over her head Uncle Charlie asked, "Could that be him approaching now?"

Jessie turned just in time to see Raine top the last boulder. Her heart leapt for joy as she faced her uncle and said simply, "Yes, that's Raine Roberts."

"You mean Caleb Robert's grandson?"

"Yes, he and his grandmother have been helping us."

"By us, you mean the rest of your siblings?"

"Yes, sir." There was a long pause as Jessie considered. "It's quite a tale and a long one at that."

Uncle Charlie looked back up as Raine approached wearing a look of concern as he hurried Thunder along. Suddenly, however, he was all smiles, as he pulled back on Thunder's reins, leapt down and approached the two.

"Charlie McAlister! Man, is it ever good to see you!" Raine reached and grabbed the man's hand and shook it soundly.

"Good to see you, too, Raine. It's been a few years. Last time I heard about you, you were in college somewhere."

"Yes, sir, but I finished up this past May and now I am back running our farm."

"Oh, Caleb's let you take over?" Uncle Charlie asked, eyebrows raised.

"Well, sir, my grandpa passed away over two years ago," Raine said softly.

Charlie looked like he was frozen in time and then tears welled up in his eyes.

"I'm sorry to break the news to you like that. I know you and he were good friends."

"I'm sorry for your loss, son, and for mine, too," was all Charlie said as he gulped hard.

Jessie shook violently about that time and Uncle Charlie came back to the present situation, "We were just going up to see if we could move that boulder and get this young'un to a warmer place."

Raine followed the finger Uncle Charlie was pointing and saw the boulder. His confusion showed on his face.

"I'll tell you what," Uncle Charlie began, "Let's check out the boulder and save our talking for later."

He tied his horse to the tree next to the little stream and continued in the direction of the boulder. Raine followed leading Thunder and glancing at Jessie inquisitively. She simply smiled and followed her uncle.

As it turned out Uncle Charlie, even with his cane, required some help to make it up to the boulder. Jessie was concerned about him, but Raine steadied him as needed and they eventually attained their goal.

Raine and Uncle Charlie, with some help from Jessie, soon realized that the boulder was too heavy for the three of them. Raine suggested the rope that was always coiled on his saddle and backtracked to where he had left Thunder. He led the stallion carefully up and over the rocks and when he had regained his previous position, he removed the rope, tying one end to Thunder and wrapping the other end securely around the back and then the front of the boulder. After tightening it sufficiently, he led Thunder slowly away to the right until the rope was taut. Uncle Charlie and Jessie stood aside as Thunder strained on the rope and the boulder was eventually pulled free of its lodging. Raine stopped the stallion and Uncle Charlie and Jessie freed the rope from the boulder. Behind them the mouth of the cave gaped open again.

Raine led Thunder back to the little tree to be tied near the other horse. When he returned Uncle Charlie and Jessie had apparently already entered the opening. He knelt and peered inside. He could see the light of Uncle Charlie's flashlight over behind a ledge. He entered and watched as the two relatives moved another small boulder and Uncle Charlie with difficulty lay prone in order to crawl through the small hole that the boulder had been covering.

Suddenly Jessie spoke up, "Uncle Charlie, maybe Raine and I should crawl through first and we can help you get up on the other side."

Charlie agreed that might be best and Raine, still looking confused, crawled through the opening after Jessie. Between the two of them they were able to help her uncle stand and Charlie raised his hand and grasped the rough rock wall as he took a moment to catch his breath.

"What is this place? Some kind of tunnel leading to another cave?" Raine asked, his curiosity getting the best of him.

Uncle Charlie reached and lit the torch that hung on the wall and in the sudden light, Raine beheld Jessie simply smiling at him with a "you'll see" look. Then she headed down the tunnel following her uncle. Raine wondered about the two as he trailed behind them.

The trio soon attained the door and Raine was obviously even more baffled. Uncle Charlie reached into his pocket and withdrew an old key and inserted it into the latch on the door, however.

"Was this the door to Charlie's house?" Raine wondered but could not reconcile the noise of a waterfall with that thought.

Suddenly Charlie had the door open with help from Raine and Jessie and Raine beheld the backside of a waterfall! As the cold mist hit their benumbed faces, Jessie shivered anew and Raine looked at her incredulously.

She helped Uncle Charlie as he stepped onto the wet rocks and they both headed in the direction of a cabin off to the left. Charlie stopped and looked carefully at what was before them and then back to Jessie.

"So this is why Kevin was so insistent I save the mountain. Well, I never!"

Jessie smiled up at her Uncle. "We've tried to take care of it and we hoped you wouldn't mind. We were in a bit of a jam at the time."

"Child, you have obviously taken care of things. You were welcome at any time, but let's get on inside and get you warmed up."

Poor Raine! The truth was finally dawning on him but he was almost too awed to take it all in. The setting was so picturesque and the view off the front porch was literally breathtaking.

Jessie opened the front door and Uncle Charlie stood for a moment taking in the sight of all of his nieces and nephews sitting peacefully on the floor playing. They could not have looked more stunned. Then they jumped to their feet and ran to the beautiful young woman at the cook stove. Her hand flew to her mouth and then dropped again to enclose the little ones gathered around her.

"Well, I'm not going to bite," Uncle Charlie said gruffly.

Jessie ushered her uncle and Raine on into the room and looking at Sarah, whose complexion had blanched, offered calmly but with obvious joy, "Sarah and all of you little ones, our prayers have been answered. Uncle Charlie has finally come home!"

Sarah moved forward slowly, with little ones in tow and stood before her uncle. Then she reached out and gently hugged him, smiling her beautiful smile as tears streamed down her face. The twins each grabbed a leg and hugged it while Katy and Annie hung back shyly and then made their way to Jessie and hugged her.

Turning around, Sarah indicated that they come and warm themselves at the fire. All three gladly did so and then Sarah gracefully turned and headed for the kitchen to put on a pot of coffee.

At that moment, the back door opened and Josh and Micah entered. They stopped in their tracks and stared at the two men in the cabin. Then the twins blurted out in unison, "Uncle Cha'lie . . . Uncle Cha'lie's come home!"

Micah looked quickly at Jessie who nodded beaming. Then both boys moved across the floor with determination and smiles as they greeted their uncle.

"Are there any more I don't know about?" Uncle Charlie asked, his voice tinged with laughter.

"No, this is all of us," Jessie laughingly replied.

Micah looked at Jessie one more time and then back to Raine. "Lo, Raine," he said, nodding his head.

Josh also greeted Raine as he recalled meeting him at the General Store. Then Jessie turned red as she realized that she had completely left Raine out.

"Sarah, kids, this is Raine Roberts. Raine, this is my sister, Sarah, little sisters Katy and Annie and I think you have already seen these two, Ryler and Tyler."

Sarah moved purposefully across the floor and reached to shake Raine's hand. She looked at Jessie and signed, "You never let on he was this handsome!"

Jessie blushed again and asked, "Should I convey your thoughts to Raine?"

Blushing furiously herself, Sarah was glad when the twins interrupted, "You has the big horse. We 'member now!"

"Yes, I have the big horse," Raine chuckled as he tousled the twins heads with his big hands.

Sarah signed to Jessie at this point asking her to see if the men would like breakfast.

Both men declined but stated that the coffee was surely smelling good.

"Please sit down when you have warmed yourselves sufficiently," Jessie stated graciously.

Uncle Charlie moved to the couch and took his seat rather stiffly. Both twins grinning mischievously, moved in unison and sat down on the couch scooting close to their uncle. He looked down at them curiously and then harrumphed. They giggled and scooted even closer.

"You boys missing your grandpa?" Uncle Charlie asked gruffly.

"Yes. We miss him lots. Jessie says he will come back someday, though."

"Well, we are going to work on getting him back with you just as soon as we can."

"Oh, boy!" The twins cried out in unison.

"Now is somebody going to tell me just how you happen to be living in my cabin?"

CHAPTER SEVENTEEN

JESSIE AND HER siblings looked at one another in silence and Uncle Charlie gazed around at the group. Finally, appearing obviously perplexed, he asked again, "How in the dickens did you find it?"

Raine looked at Jessie and grinned, "I would like to hear this myself."

Suddenly, everyone heard a whimpering and scratching at the door.

"There is one more member of the family," Jessie explained as she nodded to Micah to let Wolf in.

All anyone saw was a blur, however, as Wolf raced across the floor and jumped up on Uncle Charlie's knees and licked him immediately in the face.

"Wolf!" Jessie called out in embarrassment.

Uncle Charlie, however, hugged him close as tears started down his cheeks only to be licked off by the exuberant dog.

Everyone watched silently what was obviously a joyous reunion. When finally, Charlie could speak he explained that this was "King" the dog he had left behind three years ago. "King" was unable to contain his joy at seeing his master again and so it was a while before anyone could say much. When both had finally calmed down, Sarah signed that she had made some shortnin' bread which would be out of the oven in a few minutes and the coffee was ready to go with it. Everyone washed up and then sat around the table to eat the treat and drink the coffee and hot chocolate and tell their tales. "King" went over to Sarah and nuzzled her and then took his place at Uncle Charlie's feet.

"All right, I deserve to hear the story," Uncle Charlie stated as he looked around at each one but continued stroking King's head.

Jessie started the tale with a brief mention of their mother's passing. She deliberately left out the fact that it had been in childbirth as Annie did not know this and they had all decided to keep it from her until she was older.

Uncle Charlie gazed around at all the young ones and said softly, "I'm sorry about your mother, she was a beautiful lady."

Jessie simply mentioned, too, that they had to get away from Sean and left out the mention of the incident with Sarah and the candlestick. She told about their grandpa and how he had not been in his right mind for some time and what a miracle it was that he had come to and presented the plan to come to Charlie's.

Uncle Charlie dropped his head and a tear slowly made its way down his cheek. Kevin had come to and immediately thought of his only brother. Oh, the years they had lost!

Micah continued the story of loading up the car and making the trip up to North Carolina and the primitive campground. He praised Jessie for driving all night and still taking care of them all as they hiked up the mountain the next day.

Josh broke in and told how the twins, just two and one half years old had marched up the mountain like little Indians and had seen a "monkey" on the way. Raine and Charlie stopped and peered at his innocent look and then

Josh broke into laughter only to be joined by the twins with Ryler insisting "it was too a montey!"

Jessie explained about the chip "monkey" and then continued telling about their long hike, finally ending at the picnic rock and how exhausted everyone was. Katy piped in and told about how her doll had gotten dirty.

"You don't say!" Uncle Charlie exclaimed and Katy nodded most seriously.

"Then Micah and I walked up on Castleknob looking for you, Uncle Charlie," Jessie looked at her uncle affectionately, which was not lost on him.

"We searched high and low and then decided we would have to continue the next day and that is when Micah discovered the cave," Jessie stated proudly.

"Jessie climbed off the rocks and got the others and I collected sticks for a fire and had one going by the time the others got there," Micah continued.

"The girls, 'cept Jessie, wuz skeered of bats and snakes," the twins threw in.

Everyone laughed and Raine glanced over at Jessie with fresh admiration.

"We spent the night in the cave and then Josh, Micah and I left early the next morning to get the rest of our things out of the car."

"And on the way back up there was a really bad storm and we had to spend the night at Shelter Rock," Josh contributed.

"Micah came through again and built us another fire so it ended up being kind of cozy once our clothes and hair dried. We had food in our packs so we had dinner," Jessie continued.

"And, Josh roasted Vienna Sausages," Micah inserted grinning.

"We all ended up eating some and they were good, too!" Josh exclaimed.

"Everyone was glad to see us when we arrived back the next morning and after Grandpa had fed us pancakes Micah and I left again to get the car and take it to a chop shop."

The story telling was briefly interrupted as Sarah placed more shortnin' bread on the table and offered coffee and hot chocolate again.

"We sold the car and bought some boys clothes at their local thrift shops. At Sarah's suggestion, I stuffed my long hair under Micah's hat and have been dressing like a boy ever since for the protection of us all."

Uncle Charlie nodded with understanding as he reached for another square of the delicious dessert. "Sarah, that old cookstove has never seen anything so fine prepared in it in my day."

Sarah blushed and signed, "Thank you."

Continuing Jessie recounted the trip back on the train and buying herself some boy's clothes at the thrift shop and a dime book about kudzu which proved invaluable to them.

"Oh, yeah. You can cook with it and even make flour out of the roots," Uncle Charlie added. "But how did you find my cabin?"

"Micah and I came back up the mountain to discover that the twins were missing. We spent until after dark searching and everyone was frantic to find them."

"But we went to see the west of the tassel," Ryler spoke up importantly.

"Josh had leaned against the wall of the cave and was able to hear the twins arguing and Josh is the one who discovered the opening they had entered by. We were so glad to see that the twins were all right!" Jessie stated emphatically as she looked at the twins who were giggling to beat the band as they realized they were the center of attention.

After a pause in which everyone enjoyed the antics of their little brothers, Jessie continued, "Josh and Micah and I checked out the tunnel to see just how much danger they had been in."

"And, that's when we found the door," Josh interjected.

"Of course, as you know, it was locked," Jessie continued, looking at her uncle.

Charlie chuckled and shook his head, "I put that lock on the door for the family memories it brought me. Never thought I would be keeping family out."

"Jessie wouldn't agree to let us go back and see if Grandpa could pick the lock that night. Grandpa thought it best, too, to wait for morning so that is what we did," Micah added.

"We were up early the next day, however, and headed back to the door with Grandpa," Jessie paused and looked her uncle full in the face again.

"We thought Grandpa was slipping in his mind again when we got to the door and he pulled an old key out of his pocket," Micah continued.

Charlie chuckled and shook his head again, "And the key fit and you kids were surprised."

"Yes, how did you know?" Josh asked incredulously.

Jessie and Raine exchanged glances as Jessie continued, "Because Josh, Uncle Charlie has a key just like Grandpa's."

Josh whirled around and faced his uncle, "You do!"

"Yes, son, we both had matching keys given to us by OUR grandpa. Pretty fancy ones in our day, too."

"That is how Uncle Charlie unlocked the door today," Jessie explained.

"Unlocked the door? You came through the tunnel?" asked Micah incredulously.

"Yes, Raine used Thunder to pull the boulder away from the opening and now we can come and go that way, provided Uncle Charlie doesn't mind us continuing to live here now," Jessie looked anxiously at her uncle.

"Child, where in the world else are you going to go until we get this situation all figured out. You're certainly welcome to live on here as long as you like. That's settled!" Uncle Charlie stated emphatically.

Looking at Sarah with relief written on her face, Jessie watched as Sarah signed to her quickly, "We will move upstairs and let Uncle Charlie have his bed back."

Jessie nodded and then continued as her uncle indicated for her to keep going with her tale.

"Grandpa did unlock the door and then we all four struggled to get it open. We were shocked to see the underside of a waterfall on the other side of the door!" Jessie exclaimed.

"That was a special moment as the sun shone through the mist and the mist hit our faces," Jessie looked at Raine as she spoke and he nodded in understanding.

"We couldn't believe it when we walked out on the rocks and saw the cabin," Micah exclaimed. "It must have taken you a long time to build it."

"It did, son, but what more special setting for my home," Uncle Charlie's eyes became wistful as he remembered.

"Grandpa made us stay outside until he had checked everything out when we realized there was no smoke coming from the chimney," Micah continued.

Charlie gaged Micah's words, then nodded with understanding as he reflected that must have been difficult for his only brother.

No one spoke as they realized the significance of this moment. They had believed Uncle Charlie could possibly have been dead that day and now here he was sitting in his own cabin again.

It was still sinking in when Sarah, moving quietly, offered her uncle another piece of the shortbread as she poured him some more coffee.

Uncle Charlie thanked her and then realized he had forgotten just how good coffee perked on a wood stove could be!

"We checked everything out and then made the decision that maybe you would not mind if we sort of settled in," Jessie looked at her uncle carefully as she continued. "I mean we had the baby and all and needed a warm dry place to stay."

"Jessie, I could not be more honored that you moved into my cabin," Uncle Charlie looked around as he spoke, "You have made it homey and I had never been able to pull that off. It needed a woman's touch."

"Well, Sarah is the one to thank for that," Jessie added as she looked at her sister with a smile.

Sarah signed back rapidly and Micah translated for his uncle and Raine as he saw Jessie blushing. "Sarah says that Jessie could have done the same things, but she has been too busy keeping us all supplied with food by hiking up and down the mountain and looking for ginseng and other things to sell to keep us going."

"So you've become a 'sanghunter' have you?" Uncle Charlie asked with admiration evident in his eyes.

Jessie blushed again as she looked at Raine, "Grandpa taught me and we went together until he left and then Raine and I teamed up this fall and we have been searching the woods together towards the end of the season."

Uncle Charlie looked at Raine and then back at Jessie, "There is something I don't quite understand. If you were all safe on the mountain and had enough to eat and 'sang' to provide for you financially, then why in the world would Kevin have left and put himself in such jeopardy?"

Suddenly the older siblings looked uncomfortable and Jessie glanced down and traced a pattern on the tablecloth. Raine spoke up carefully at this point. "Charlie . . . it came out in the paper that you were behind on your taxes and your property was about to be auctioned off. Apparently, when the family realized that they could not raise enough money in time to save your place, your brother left the mountain to go back home and withdraw his savings in order to pay your taxes."

Uncle Charlie looked intently into the faces of the older siblings. "So Kevin had no choice but to leave," he said softly as he stroked his chin, "he had to save the mountain for me and you. If it sold, the new owners could have come up here and perhaps discovered your whereabouts eventually. Hmm."

"We believed in our hearts that you were still alive and we certainly did not want to see you lose your place if we could help it, especially after it had sheltered us in our time of need," Jessie responded softly.

Tears flowed freely down Uncle Charlie's face now. He seemed deeply touched by what his brother had done for them all.

"We have some work to do, children," Uncle Charlie breathed out as, with effort, he composed himself.

"Jessie and Raine found a lot of ginseng and Jessie's part might help," Micah offered.

Raine spoke up at this point, "I would be willing to help, too, though even pooling our resources, I'm afraid we will still be a little short."

Uncle Charlie's face contorted once again, "That's mighty neighborly of you Raine. I would hate for you to do that and for myself, I would just let the mountain go . . ."

Protests quickly arose from his nieces and nephews, but Uncle Charlie put up his hand and continued, "but that would not be in the best interests of you children. The savings I have are already promised to pay on my bill at the nursing home and frankly they'll be eyeing my property as soon as they find out about it."

Silence ensued as this last bombshell sunk in.

Raine glanced around at everyone's stricken faces and then as a way to encourage and dissipate the gloom, offered, "Charlie, I would say we just need to pay a visit to the courthouse today and see exactly what we are up against with the taxes, especially since the auction is scheduled for tomorrow. Maybe they will give you some kind of forbearance given your situation and all. But we don't need to delay in addressing things. Are you up to a trip back down the mountain today?"

"I'm tougher than I look," Uncle Charlie stated emphatically as he raised his chin. He arose stiffly and then turned back to face everyone. "We'll talk about your grandpa when I get back and see what we can do about getting him released."

This statement was met with smiles from his family and he gazed upon each face and then made his way to the mantel and slowly caressed his dad's old clock. He opened the front and reached his hand carefully up behind the inner workings. Withdrawing a piece of paper folded in half he paused and just gazed at it as his family and Raine looked on curiously.

Then with care he unfolded the paper and perused its contents. His eyes filled with tears as he read:

> *Charlie, if you are reading this then that means that you have returned and I am not there for whatever reason. I wanted to thank you for the use of your cabin and how it has provided shelter and protection for my grandchildren and me. I have not ceased to admire your cleverness and ingenuity since living here. I appreciate you, my brother, and want you to know that if something should happen to me, I would feel blessed if you would take over the care of my grandchildren, your own nieces and nephews. I know you would grow to love them and they you.*
>
> *I bequeath them to your care,*
>
> *Your brother, forever, Kevin*

Uncle Charlie stood for what seemed like an eternity just gazing at the paper with tears in his eyes. Finally, Jessie could stand it no longer and moved to his side.

"Uncle Charlie, is everything all right," she asked softly.

He raised his tear-rimmed eyes to look at her and replied, "Your grandpa and I used to leave each other notes in the back of this old clock when we were growing up."

He paused and took a deep breath before continuing, "When I visited him yesterday, he told me to look in the clock and now I see why. He knew I hadn't forgotten the good times we used to have or the bond we shared."

Looking over Jessie's head at Raine, he said, "Well, I guess we must be going. We've got a lot to take care of today."

Stuffing the paper into his shirt pocket, he turned and watched as King made his way to his old master's side. "I'll be back, King, and you and I will share more good times together, Lord willing."

So saying, Uncle Charlie patted King's upturned head affectionately and made for the door. King stood and watched as the man who had raised him from a pup left with Raine and Jessie at his side. Then he turned and headed back to Sarah, who kneeled and hugged him as tears streamed down her cheeks.

CHAPTER EIGHTEEN

JESSIE SAW THE men to the mouth of the cave and then assuring them of her prayers turned to make her way back through the tunnel.

Reaching the door at the other end, Jessie paused a moment to stroke its familiar rough beams. She found she had missed going through this old tunnel. It had reflected safety to them all and she was ever so thankful to be using it again. She knew the exit they had used through the kudzu would grow back to its old self next year and no one would suspect the bare vines at its end of hiding anything this fall and winter. It had been the painstaking pulling herself through at the end that had posed so much danger. Now that was over. God had answered some of their greatest concerns and in what a way!

Uncle Charlie was alive and had returned! He would help them with Grandpa's situation. He would take responsibility for saving the mountain now. A huge weight had been lifted off her shoulders. She breathed deeply releasing the tension and embracing the joy that flooded in as the mist caressed her face when she opened the door.

She stood and let that glorious feeling pervade her soul until her face became numb from the cold. Then she made her way to the warmth of the cabin and found another joyous celebration as she entered its coziness.

Sarah had all of the children holding hands and going round and round in the middle of the room. They were giggling to beat the band and then they all dropped to the floor as if on cue. Sarah was smiling from ear to ear as she raised her eyes and beheld Jessie's reddened face.

Jessie, however, let her know it was nothing to be concerned about. She had just been enjoying herself in the mist of the waterfall. Then she dropped to the floor and tried to kiss each child with her cold lips. Of course, that started more laughter as the children made every effort to escape from her.

What wonderful, simple times, Jessie thought, as she relished each moment. Was it not right to celebrate Uncle Charlie's return?

Sarah caught two of the little ones and held them close and then set them free in order to sign that she must get up and begin preparation for the evening meal. They would have a feast to celebrate Uncle Charlie's return.

"Well, actually, Sarah, Uncle Charlie is not going to be coming back up here today. Raine has invited him to stay with him and his grandmother. He thought three trips up and down the mountain might be too much for Uncle Charlie and so our uncle will be staying with the Roberts tonight. They are going to discuss what they will be told at the courthouse today regarding the auction and attempt to save the mountain and, of course, what can be done about Grandpa's situation."

As Jessie saw a look of disappointment cross Sarah's face, she hurried on, "I really think this is for the best. Uncle Charlie has been dealt some blows and surprises just one after another since he remembered who he is and even with riding a horse, the trip up and down the mountain must be hard on him after his injuries and convalescence."

Slowly Sarah nodded her agreement and then signed that they should celebrate anyway. She would save the "feast" for later, but they would have a special cake for tonight. All the kids yelled, "Hooray!" and pounced on Sarah so that she fell backwards on the floor from her sitting position. Her silent laughter could be felt if not heard and Jessie laughed out loud with pure joy.

Finally, Sarah, with tears streaming down her face from how hard she had laughed, pushed the children back and rose to her feet. She brushed off her dress, signing quickly that she had to get to work if she was going to have dinner ready and bake a cake, too.

Jessie offered her help and the two started their preparations, but the relief in the cabin was palpable.

CHAPTER NINETEEN

"WELL, CHARLIE MCALISTER! You are a sight for sore eyes!" Nattie exclaimed as she opened her kitchen door and watched as Charlie climbed the two steps. Then she moved forward and embraced him soundly.

As Nattie stepped back and continued to grasp Charlie's arms, she noted the tears in his eyes as her own ran freely down her face. "I wasn't sure if we would ever see you again, but I can't tell you how glad I am that we are."

"It's good to see you, too, Nattie. I was awfully sorry to hear the news about Caleb's death, though. I'll surely miss him. He was a good friend," Charlie's sincerity was obvious and so was his changed condition as Nattie stepped aside and welcomed him, once again, into her home.

"It was hard losing him and it is still hard being without him, but Raine has accepted the responsibility of running the farm and is doing a fine job," Nattie glanced at Raine with pride shining from her eyes.

"Please sit down and I'll get you a cup of coffee," Nattie indicated her kitchen table and immediately grabbed three mugs.

"As I recall, you take yours black," setting the big mug in front of her guest and pouring it full, Nattie placed the other two and poured the rich brew into them. Then she turned to put a pound cake on the table in front of Charlie. Slicing a generous portion and putting it on a plate for him, she saw his eyes widen.

"You'll make me fat," Charlie complained good-naturedly.

"Well, you need to be fattened up some. You've lost considerable weight since I last saw you and you did not need to lose any then."

Charlie smiled and looked across the checkered table, "Does she treat you this way, too, Raine?"

"Oh, yes sir, and sometimes worse. If I don't eat my share around here you would think it was the end of the world," Raine smiled and winked at his grandma.

"Psshaw! Both of you could use fattening up!" Nattie returned in mock indignation.

"Grandma, I have invited Charlie to stay the night . . ."

"Well, of course, he is spending this night and as many more as he needs. Our home is open to you, Charlie, and if you will stay long enough, I will get that meat back on your bones."

Charlie grinned and then expressed his gratitude.

"Now, tell me what you can about what happened since the day you left," Nattie began with eagerness in her voice.

"Well, there is not much to tell," began Uncle Charlie as he traced a pattern on the tablecloth with his index finger.

Looking at Nattie's expectant face, however, he decided to oblige her, "I got to thinking one day sitting on the mountain that it was probably time I made out a will. I thought I would see some long lost relatives, as well, so I made my plans, got everything ready and left. I made it to Ninety Six, got off the bus, toured around town for a couple of hours and was struck by a truck. Apparently, from what I was told later, I barely survived the injuries. I received a severe blow to my old hard noggin and it literally knocked me senseless. I was admitted to the nursing facility eventually since no one knew what to do with me and there I remained until a few days ago recovering from my injuries."

Charlie paused to take a deep breath, "I immediately sought out Kevin when I left, after seeing the article in the paper and all. It's ironic that Kevin's incarceration and the write-up actually set me free. I don't know if I would ever have recalled anything if I had not seen that newspaper. Anyhow, it was so good to see Kevin again after such a long separation. Kevin, however, did not seem all that worried about himself, but he did impress upon me how imperative it was to save the mountain. Of course, I did not know why until I arrived there. I have family living in my old cabin. Who would have ever believed that?"

Nattie nodded, "It is interesting how it has all worked out so far. God orchestrated it just so, didn't He?"

Charlie nodded as a faraway look crossed his face.

"How did you meet up with Raine?" Nattie continued.

"I had rented a horse to get up the mountain and when I arrived at the top I saw what I thought was a young man hiding behind a boulder. As it turned out, it was Jessie hiding back there half freezing to death, waiting for Raine. He showed up shortly after that little gal and I got acquainted again. We all went to the cabin then and had quite a family reunion. Didn't know I had so many nieces and nephews."

Nattie smiled broadly and then looked at Raine with affection.

"Anyway, Raine, here took me to the courthouse after all that and we presented our case. They were sympathetic and that has bought me a couple more weeks. At least, that gives us a little time to deal with this situation and get our bearings regarding Kevin," Charlie explained.

"Oh, it's such a shame about Kevin! Anyone who knows him could tell you he would never do such a thing!" Nattie's eyes blazed her indignation as she speared another bite of pound cake.

"Irregardless, he is in a heap of trouble and I'm not sure just how we can get him out, short of turning the kids over to the authorities and letting them have their say," Charlie rejoined.

"Well, we certainly can't do that. The authorities would have those poor children separated up into foster homes in the blink of an eye. Of course, they mean well, but those kids need to be together and remain a family," Nattie stated emphatically.

"I would take responsibility for them myself legally, but I don't believe the authorities would allow that with me having no visible means of support and where I live and all, not counting my recent past," Charlie shook his head as he took another bite of the delicious pound cake followed by a big gulp of hot coffee.

"I've thought about applying for their guardianship myself, but then we have the issue of knowing about their whereabouts and not reporting it to the authorities. I don't like all of this secrecy but I see no other way around the dilemma," Nattie looked up at Raine suddenly who was looking very pensive.

"Son, you've been awfully quiet since you got back. Is everything all right?"

Glancing at his grandma quickly, Raine turned crimson and stammered, "I have just been trying to reason through everything."

Continuing to stare at her grandson, Nattie, who could read him like a book, knew something was on his mind. He was probably just hesitant to say anything in front of Charlie.

"I wish I had told Jessie to meet me at the boulder this evening. I know she would like to know about the postponement of the auction."

"Well, why don't you just head on back up there and knock on the door," Charlie asked in his matter-of-fact way.

"As you already know, I just learned about your method of entry this morning and Jessie has never told me I could use it," Raine continued.

"Well, I'm telling you to use it. I would like to take your grandma up on her offer of hospitality at least for another night. I want to go down tomorrow and meet with Kevin's lawyer and might not be up to riding back up the mountain so soon after that, besides I'm not sure but what he might need me to do some things for him. I'd like the kids to know I will be back up when I can."

"If you're sure, then I will head on out so I won't be getting back too late," Raine began, only to be cut off by Charlie.

"Here, Son. You'll need this," Charlie reached in his pocket and extracted his keys with a little difficulty. He removed the skeleton key and handed it to Raine.

"Guard this well and you can use it until I need it back."

Raine took the proffered key as if it was a treasure, which in his mind it was. He was ecstatic that he would actually be able to go calling on Jessie at her own front door.

Nattie did not miss the look of joy that crossed Raine's face and turned to address Charlie, "That's mighty nice of you, Charlie. I don't know just what ya'll are talking about, but I am sure someone will fill me in later if I need to know."

"I will oblige you, but right now I think this young man is eager to be underway."

Raine arose from the table and shook Charlie's hand in gratitude as Nattie went to fetch some more supplies she was sending to Jessie and her family.

Leaving the two with their talking and planning, Raine saddled Thunder, packed the supplies and headed back up the mountain. Wouldn't Jessie be surprised?

CHAPTER TWENTY

ARRIVING AT CASTLEKNOB a little after 4:00 PM, Raine felt uncharacteristically nervous. He tied Thunder to the tree next to the spring and made his way to the cave. Carefully scouting the area to make sure he was alone, he dropped down into the cave's opening. Shining his flashlight around the perimeter, he thought again of Jessie and how very brave she had been to come and go in this manner for so long. He hugged the wall of the cave as he had been instructed to do in order to leave no footprints in the fine dust. Locating the small boulder which hid the opening to the tunnel, he made his way into the interior of the mountain.

Wending his way back through the tunnel, he at length approached the large wooden door and withdrew Charlie's skeleton key. He inserted it and pulled it back some as he turned it just like he had seen Charlie do. Sure enough he heard the inner workings click and with some effort he opened the heavy door and felt the rush of mist from the waterfall hit his face. He shivered involuntarily as it was a chilly day already without the cold mist. Once again, he thought about Jessie and how many times this had happened to her.

Making his way to the cabin door, his apprehension mounted. Would Jessie think it was all right that he had come? He certainly hoped so, and in a few moments he would know for sure.

Taking a deep breath, he knocked gently. The chatter he had heard on the inside ceased immediately and there was a running of little feet towards what he knew to be the kitchen area. Then ever so slowly, the door opened and Jessie stuck her head around it while clinging to its roughness. He could see the shock register in her eyes as she beheld who it was and then she blushed furiously and looked quickly around Raine.

Guessing her intent, Raine immediately sought to set her mind at ease, "Your Uncle Charlie is not with me. He wanted me to come and deliver a message to you."

"Raine, forgive me, please come in out of the cold," Jessie stepped back and opened the door in welcome, "I am totally unaccustomed to anyone knocking on this door. It took me back a little."

"I can fully understand that," Raine responded as he entered the coziness of the cabin and relaxed some.

He looked beyond Jessie to Sarah, whose face was flushed from her meal preparation. The little ones were clinging to her apron and she had shielded them with her arms not knowing just who was knocking at their door. She smiled broadly, however, and signed something to Jessie, then bent to pick up Annie who hid her curly red head behind Sarah's ash blond braids which she had wrapped around her perfectly shaped head.

"Sarah wants to know if you will stay for dinner. We are having a special celebration tonight in honor of Uncle Charlie's return. It includes cake," Jessie smiled, her gray-green eyes twinkling.

"Oh, I don't . . ." Raine began, then thought perhaps that would not be such a bad idea after all.

"I've partaken of your hospitality, remember," Jessie asked with a mischievous look on her face.

"That you have and I would be remiss if I did not take an opportunity to enjoy your sister's wonderful cooking again," Raine returned, looking at Sarah.

Sarah blushed but smiled with pleasure and mouthed, "Thank you."

"Then its settled. Won't you have a seat?" Jessie asked graciously.

"Thank you, I will, but first I need to divest myself of this pack. Grandma sent some things that she thought you might be able to use," Raine replied as he carried the pack to the kitchen where he emptied the items for Sarah to put away. He returned to the living area and sat down close to the fireplace.

Jessie noted the items Raine's grandma had sent and thanked Raine profusely for them while Sarah signed her thanks. Raine saw how excited they both were to receive what had been sent and guessed that these items must have been an answer to their prayers.

"You said you have a message," Jessie stated, returning to sit down near Raine after an awkward silence.

"Yes, your Uncle Charlie wanted you to know that he will be staying with my grandma and me for a few days. He plans to visit the lawyer tomorrow and I really think the trip up and down the mountain today was a little much for him after his recent release from the nursing facility."

"I was concerned about that myself. I'm secretly relieved as I did not want him to overdo. Of course, when he is ready, he can certainly move back into his own cabin," Jessie replied.

"It was your Uncle Charlie's idea for me to come knock on your door. He supplied me with his skeleton key so I could come through the tunnel."

"I surmised that much since it would have been pretty much impossible for you to have gotten here any other way."

At that, Raine looked at Jessie quizzically. "I will explain some other time," Jessie replied as the little ones finally made their way to the two adults and giggled and smiled to beat the band.

The next twenty minutes or so were spent entertaining the twins, Katie and Annie as they were wired up from all of the company they had had today after over two and one half years without any.

Raine found himself enjoying Jessie's little siblings immensely. He had never been around many kids having grown up an only child and had only interacted some with the children at church on occasion. These were bright little ones and were warming up to him nicely. It was obvious that they adored their older sister, Jessie, and the love she had for them shone out of her eyes.

Eventually, Sarah signed that it was time for her little brothers and sisters to run to the barn and fetch Micah and Josh for dinner. That gave Raine and Jessie a few moments to discuss what had transpired at the courthouse. Jessie was certainly relieved that they had been given a little more time. Maybe the ginseng would be dry by then thus fetching a higher price.

Raine lowered his voice and asked Jessie what he had been wanting to ask since he arrived. "Could I see you alone after our meal?"

"I think that could be arranged. I'll walk with you to the tunnel," Jessie replied softly.

Micah and Josh entered the back door with the little ones running in ahead of them. Micah's eyebrows were immediately raised at sight of Raine, but he was cordial. Josh on the other hand seemed genuinely pleased to see Jessie's friend.

Everyone got in line to wash up and Raine noted that all of the siblings helped one another. It was very obvious that they were a close-knit family.

Jessie got Micah aside while the little ones were finishing up and relayed the good news about the auction to him. He was visibly relieved.

Sarah indicated that Raine was to be seated beside Jessie and when everyone had taken their places, nodded to Micah to ask the blessing.

"Our dear, heavenly Father, we thank you again so very much for your provision of our food. We thank you for Raine who has been taking his time and energy to deliver it to us and for the generosity of both he and his grandma. We thank you for Uncle Charlie's homecoming and that he has recovered so well from his accident. We thank you for protecting us and for all of your blessings upon us and we ask that you would be with Grandpa and our dad, wherever he is right now and we know you will bring them both back to us in your good timing. It is in the name of your dear Son, Jesus, that we pray."

All of the children said "Amen" in unison with Micah and Raine raised his head to find everyone looking his way.

He glanced quickly at Jessie to see what this meant and she laughed, "You are our guest and they are waiting for you to go first."

Raine reddened and then grinned, "Since everyone looks hungry, I had better get to it."

Sarah passed the pot roast to him and then signed something to Jessie.

"Sarah wanted me to thank you and your grandma for the provision of the pot roast. That is not something we have as a rule," Jessie offered by way of explanation.

"Well, we have plenty in our freezer so I will see that you have some again soon," Raine replied.

The little one's plates were helped and it was obvious that they were enjoying the meal immensely. Raine had to admit that except for a little reserve on Micah's part, everyone was treating him like family. The children were full of questions and he entertained them with tales of his adventures on Thunder. They squealed with delight from time to time and he smiled to think he had pleased them. What a wonderful family Jessie had and how he loved spending this time with them.

All too soon the meal ended and the family seemed truly disappointed that Raine needed to head on back home.

Jessie told them she would walk out with Raine and that she would be back soon. That said, the twosome headed out into the cold towards the waterfall. The sky was a riot of colors from the sunset and as they reached the waterfall and looked through it at the evening display, it literally took their breath away. What a special day this had been! And now, to end on such a colorful note.

Suddenly Raine grasped both of Jessie's hands and held them close to his chest as they faced one another beneath the waterfall. "Jessie, I have been praying about something and this afternoon I believe I received my answer. Would you do me the honor of becoming my wife?"

That was the last thing Jessie had expected hearing and the thing she had wanted most to hear. It was so magical beneath the waterfall even with the cold mist in their faces that for a moment she was not sure she trusted her ears. She looked deeply into Raine's eyes with stars dancing in her own.

Then she heard Raine ask, "Well?"

"Raine, you have just made me the happiest woman on the face of this earth. Of course, I want to be your wife! The answer is yes!"

Slowly Raine released her hands and slid his arms around her shoulders and then gently laid his lips against her cold forehead then placed another gentle kiss upon her nose and then moved to her lips. He was literally lost in a sea of love, totally oblivious to the cold until he felt Jessie shiver.

"You're cold," he breathed softly.

"That could be one of the reasons," Jessie returned with a glint of happiness in her eyes.

"Jessie, we have a lot to discuss and I would like to pick you up tomorrow and take you to my house so that we can make our plans where you will be warmer. Would that be possible?"

"What time were you thinking?" Jessie asked with bated breath.

"How about ten? I think Charlie and Grandma are going down to see the lawyer tomorrow, so we will have the house to ourselves. We can have our discussion over lunch. Does that sound all right?" Raine looked at Jessie intently, awaiting her reply.

"Are you sure it will be safe for me to leave the mountain?"

"You just dress warmly and I will make sure you are safe," Raine responded as he drew her into a protective hug.

"All right, then I will see you at 10:00," Jessie lifted her chin as she took Raine at his word. Somehow she knew it would be all right.

Kissing her once more on the forehead, Raine turned and made his way into the tunnel pulling the heavy door behind him and locking it with the treasured skeleton key. He wasn't sure whether his feet were touching the ground or not as he made his way back to Thunder. All he did know was that he must be the most blessed man that ever walked on air.

CHAPTER TWENTY-ONE

THE SECOND JESSIE walked back into the cabin, Sarah knew something had happened. She had never seen Jessie look so happy in all of her life. Walking past her gaping sister, Jessie made her way into their bedroom where she draped herself across the bed.

Sarah entered close on her sister's heels. She noted the joyful flush upon her face and her eyes looked as if they held a thousand stars. Sarah sat down upon the end of the bed and signed, "Well?"

Grabbing her pillow and hugging it close, Jessie turned on her back and gazed at the ceiling then she looked back at her sister, "Raine asked me to marry him."

Sarah's eyes became as big as saucers and her smile was full of joy as she signed, "Did you give him the right answer?"

"Well, if you are angling for a brother-in-law I did," Jessie laughingly replied.

If Jessie had ever heard a silent squeal, it was now. Sarah leaned across the bed and hugged her sister soundly, then pushed her back and signed, "Well, tell me all about it."

"There is really not much to tell," Jessie began, knowing the response she would get as she was playfully hit with a pillow.

"Oh, Sarah, we were standing under the waterfall with the sunset shining through. It was so spectacular! He had prayed about asking me and had just gotten the answer this afternoon. We are going to meet in the morning and go to his house and iron out all of the details. I can hardly wait and I bet I will not be able to sleep one whit tonight," Jessie reclined back on the bed in a luxurious manner, her eyes still full of light.

Sarah drew her feet up onto the bed and clasped her knees, laying her head upon them and looking at Jessie. Then she unclasped her hands and signed, "I just knew this was going to happen. I felt when you first told me about him that he was the one for you. He fit in so well with the family this afternoon, too. I cannot wait to meet his grandma! Should we invite her up?"

"I don't know. I will discuss that with Raine tomorrow, but it would be very nice if we could. Oh, there are so many details to work out. Our situation won't make that easy, but somehow things will happen so that I can become Mrs. Raine Roberts!"

Sarah laughed her silent laugh and then signed with consternation, "Shouldn't you tell the others?"

"I just wanted a few minutes to revel in this joy before I met with any opposition, if you know what I mean," Jessie replied soberly.

"Would you like me to tell Micah?" Sarah signed after some thought.

"No, I think it should come from me, though I appreciate your thoughtfulness, Sarah."

"I want to think some things through first, before I let everyone else know," Jessie said softly as she reclined upon the bed once again.

"I will leave you alone then with your thoughts," Sarah signed and then arose gracefully and returned to the living area.

Jessie lay in a state of bliss as she considered the afternoon and evening and all that it meant and just how it had changed her life. Of course, their situation was unchanged, but somehow Jessie knew that even if things did not work out the way they all planned, it would still be all right. They were in God's very capable hands, after all.

Then she turned her thoughts to Raine exclusively. God had brought this man into her life and she could not have been more certain that he was the one chosen for her. Her heart was full to overflowing with love for her intended. She thought of the shrub, hearts-a-burstin', and knew now how that name felt.

Finally, the sounds of the cabin filtered through Jessie's thoughts and she realized that Sarah was taking care of getting the children ready for bed. She needed to get up and do her part and she wanted to relay her wonderful news. But how good it felt just to lie there and swim in that sea of love!

Jessie gave in to duty's call eventually and arose to help her sister. The twins had already had their baths and were sitting on the couch lost in their own little world of giggling over something silly. Micah was learning a new song on Uncle Charlie's fiddle and Josh was lying on the quilt on the floor rereading an old paperback.

Looking at each beloved sibling, Jessie took a deep breath as Sarah entered the living room behind the freshly scrubbed Katy and Annie. Sarah nodded her support and Jessie knew it was time.

"Everyone, please listen for a moment. I have something to tell you," Jessie began.

As everything quieted down, Jessie locked eyes with Micah, "I wanted you all to know that Raine has asked me to marry him."

Micah's eyebrows went up and he opened his mouth to speak, but the cheers from his other siblings left him mute for the moment.

The little ones and Josh jumped up and ran to Jessie, hugging her and expressing their delight in their individual ways. The twins were jumping around like little Indians and Josh was just about as wild. The girls could not quit hugging their sister but through it all, Jessie noticed a look pass between Sarah and Micah.

As things calmed down some, Micah rose to his feet and everyone looked his way.

"What was your answer, Jessie?"

"Micah, I have loved Raine pretty much from the first time I saw him. I believe God brought him into my life and yours. He has been chosen for me. How could I answer anything but 'yes'?" Jessie asked as the stars still shone from her eyes.

"Well, I cannot argue with that answer. It would seem we are going to have a new brother-in-law," Micah smiled slightly, then crossed the floor and gave Jessie a brotherly hug.

All of the children squealed at his comment and the twins started a wild cavort with Ryler saying over and over again, "a new brover-in law, a new brover-in-law!"

When things quieted down at last and the little ones fell in an exhausted heap on the quilt, Sarah took charge and ushered them all off to bed.

Jessie, still standing, locked eyes with Micah once again.

"Micah, I truly hope you understand."

Micah dropped his eyes to the floor and after a long pause, lifted them once again and said softly, "Jessie, I do not believe you would ever do anything to interfere with my happiness if it was me who had found that special someone and I have no intention of interfering with yours."

Pure joy shone from Jessie's eyes as it sunk in just what Micah was saying and she fairly flew across the floor to hug her brother again.

"Micah, I cannot thank you enough for your support! Please know that Raine and I will take great care to continue to protect this family and keep everyone together. Somehow, I believe it is going to be for the best for everyone, not just Raine and me."

"Whatever happens, Jessie, I am behind you and you deserve to be happy after all you have already done to keep us together. I hope your marriage will make things a little easier on you. You have certainly borne many burdens for all of us."

"Thank you. Micah, that means more to me than you will ever know. I think there is a reason that God brought Raine into our lives when He did and only time will show us His true wisdom."

"Speaking of time, Sarah told me that you are planning a trip off the mountain tomorrow. I am assuming it is to discuss plans with Raine?"

"That and to get more supplies. I will be careful, though. We are only going to Raine's grandmother's farm. I will see Uncle Charlie, as well, later in the day and find out just what his plans are, too."

"Sounds good. If you are going to be leaving in the morning you will need a good night's rest so I am off to bed and I suggest you do the same. You might not get much sleep, you know."

With that, Micah smiled a genuine smile of affection and left the room.

Jessie whispered "good-night" and headed to her room, where, indeed, she had great difficulty sleeping.

CHAPTER TWENTY-TWO

THE NEXT MORNING found Jessie up early in spite of her lack of sleep. She was going to spend most of the day with Raine and settle some things so she was immensely excited.

Sarah, once again, took care of most of Jessie's chores so that she could get ready and leave early to meet Raine. A knock on the door surprised them all, however, and when Jessie approached the door with trepidation and opened it, she was surprised to see Raine standing there.

"I hope you don't mind, but I wanted to pick my fiancée up at her door," a grinning Raine explained.

Before Jessie could answer the children swarmed around her and greeted their new "brover-in-law" as Ryler put it.

Blushing furiously, Jessie quickly explained that she and Raine had to be married first before he would be their new brother-in-law.

"Well, when ya gonna get married?" asked Tyler seriously.

"We are going to be deciding that soon," Jessie, still blushing, responded.

"Well, what we 'posed to call 'im?" Ryler asked just as seriously.

Katy spoke up at this point in a most authoritative way with her little hands on her hips, "He's her 'beau' brothers!"

"Well, good morning, Mr. Bo," Tyler grinned and shook Raine's hand ceremoniously.

Jessie just shook her head, grabbed her backpack and ushered Raine out the door.

As they stepped off the porch, however, the door opened slightly and Ryler called loudly, "Good-bye, Mithter Bo."

Raine and Jessie both burst out laughing as they saw Sarah pull the twins back in and gently close the door.

Jessie felt pure joy as the two descended the mountain. The fact that Raine had come to the door to pick her up was very special to her. She had certainly not expected that!

Oh, to get off the mountain again was so freeing. She apparently needed to get out more than her siblings. They all seemed perfectly content to live their lives completely on the mountain. She, on the other hand, had an intense need to, at least, see other adults on a regular basis. Maybe it was because she was older or maybe she just needed some social contact more. At any rate, she was more than happy to be going off the mountain today and that she was going with Raine made it all perfect.

Being so deep in thought Jessie was surprised when Raine turned at the shortcut. He had told her he was being extra cautious so they would not be talking on the way down. Her mind was so full of thoughts and plans, however, that she had not been too disappointed with this news. After all, she would have hours to talk to Raine once they reached his home. It had indeed been a short trip to Jessie's way of thinking.

Once they reached the farm, Raine ushered Jessie on into the house and then returned to take care of Thunder. Jessie occupied herself by listening to Raine's grandmother's little bird. She recognized it immediately as a goldfinch. It apparently had a broken wing and Jessie wondered how it had come to live in the beautiful cage in their home.

Raine was back before long and washed up before he came into the main part of the house. He pulled a chair out at the breakfast table for Jessie and they both sat down facing each other.

Raine reached across the table and took Jessie's hands into his own, "Jessie, you have made me the happiest man alive. I cannot believe you have agreed to spend the rest of your life with me."

Jessie blushed and stars shown in her eyes as she replied softly, "I cannot believe you asked me. It is more than I could ever have hoped or dreamed."

"We have some issues to work out, but I believe that we are going to have a very special life together," Raine responded as he looked deeply into Jessie's eyes.

"I am sorry I am bringing all of this . . ." began Jessie, but Raine interrupted.

"Please don't say you are sorry. I knew the score before I asked you. There are problems and huge ones at that, but nothing we cannot work out if we ask God about it and follow His leading."

Jessie smiled her gratitude at Raine but before she could speak he continued.

"What kind of wedding were you hoping to have, Jessie, and please be honest? What are your dreams for your wedding day and don't think of impossibilities right now?"

Pausing, Jessie looked into the distance, the distant future that was. What was she hoping to look back on someday?

"Well," Jessie began hesitantly, looking deeply into Raine's eyes, "I guess I am no different from other young women. I would like to be married in a white wedding gown. Nothing particularly fancy or expensive. Sarah and I could even make it. Sarah is quite the seamstress you know."

"Okay, and what else?"

"I would like my family to be there and yours, of course."

"What about a church wedding?"

"I had always envisioned that, but it is not absolutely necessary."

"I am asking what you would like, Jessie, not just what will do."

After pausing thoughtfully for a moment, Jessie smilingly replied, "Then I would like a church wedding, but I don't see how . . ."

"Uh, uh, uh," Raine interrupted, "Remember I was asking for your dreams."

Jessie smiled a radiant smile, "Then I would like punch and cake and flowers, too, at my church wedding."

"What else?"

"That pretty much sums up what I would have in the wedding of my dreams," Jessie responded with a happy sigh.

"Jessie, I think all of that could be arranged. It might take planning and a promise from my pastor for secrecy, but you are only asking for a simple church wedding and I believe that is entirely possible.

"What about you, Raine, what were you hoping for in a wedding day?"

"My fondest desire has been to marry the woman of my dreams and that, my dear, is going to happen. As far as the trappings are concerned, I leave that to the discretion of my bride-to-be," Raine smiled broadly and leaned across the table to place a kiss affectionately on Jessie's forehead.

"Now, on to the time frame. I do have some hopes there and that is to marry you as soon as is humanly possible."

Jessie came back down to earth at that comment. How could she possibly marry Raine and either come to live with him or have him live on the mountain with her family? That did seem an impossibility.

Seeing the look on her face, Raine continued, "Jessie, I have been doing a lot of thinking and praying. And, please, just hear me out."

"I think you and I should marry as soon as possible and immediately file for legal custody of your sisters and brothers. Everyone could come to live here at the farmhouse."

Seeing Jessie's protest rising to her lips, he laid a restraining finger across them and continued, "My grandma and I discussed this at length last night when I told her you had agreed to marry me and she is all for everyone coming to live here. Actually, she would really love it."

"Don't you see, Jessie, this should get your grandpa off the hook and finally released from jail where he did not deserve to be in the first place."

Jessie was stunned. Marrying Raine had seemed a remote dream and she knew that one day that would happen, but he had put so much thought into resolving her issues that her mind could not take it all in at once.

Her grandpa released from jail and back with them? Could it be that something that would bring her the greatest of joys could also bring her grandpa back to them again?

Jessie put her hands up to her face. She needed time to think this all through and certainly to pray it through.

With joy bubbling up in her at the thought of release from the prison of being discovered and having the family reunited again, she looked at Raine, her eyes big with wonder.

"You would be willing to do that for me and my family?"

"Jessie, I love you so much and I am already growing to love your family. That is really not asking that much of me," Raine's eyes glinted as he laughed a happy laugh.

"But you have lived as an only child with your grandparents all of your life. Do you really know what you are getting into with this many children?" Jessie asked as she looked at him incredulously.

"All my life I have wanted a large family. Who would have believed that marrying the girl of my dreams would give me that instantly?"

Jessie laughed with delight. Could this really be happening? Then she sobered. "Raine, I think we need to talk to a lawyer and see if this would really work. I truly want what is best for you and I'm uneasy that your knowing about our situation and not going to the authorities right away could get you into trouble."

Looking deeply into her eyes, Raine weighed her words carefully.

"Jessie, that is a risk I am willing to take, but if it would make you feel easier about everything, I will visit a lawyer. I do not believe that you, however, should go with me. It is still too risky at this point in time."

"Maybe you are right. It is hard to know what to do."

Then Jessie paused thoughtfully, "Actually, we can know exactly what to do. We just need to ask God."

At that, Raine reached across the table and gently grasped Jessie's hands. "It means a lot to me that I am marrying a woman who has such great faith. You are right, we do need to ask God."

Raine bowed his head at that point and prayed, "Our gracious Father in heaven, You already know about the issues with which we are grappling. You already know the steps we should be taking. We desperately want to do things Your way and we desperately want to keep this family together. Please show us - light the way before us and help us to discern your leading. We will give you the glory for your answers. It is in the name of your most precious Son that we pray. Amen."

Looking up with tears welling in her eyes, Jessie felt her heart swell to near bursting again with love for this man whom God had brought into her life. How could she doubt God when He had given her such a treasure?

"Are you ready for our meal," Raine asked as he glanced at the clock and realized just how the morning had gotten away from them.

"If you will point the way, I will get it on the table for us," Jessie answered.

"The dishes are in that cabinet, the glasses over there and . . . well, just ramble in the drawers for everything else," Raine moved to the refrigerator as he spoke and began putting the food that needed to be heated on the stove.

Jessie set the table and poured their drinks as her eyes grew large at the sight of all the food.

"My goodness, your grandmother must cook all the time! What a feast!"

"Well, hopefully, Grandmother and your uncle will show up soon and join us, but even if they don't, Grandmother would have prepared all of this for just the two of us. Each day is a celebration with her, you know."

Jessie helped stir the vegetables as Raine continued to bring the cold foods to the table. Suddenly, she realized just how much at home she felt in this kitchen. Actually, their entire farm felt warm and welcoming to her.

Raine announced that all was in readiness and they sat down for their first meal, with the exception of their picnics, for just the two of them. That really felt different to Jessie who was accustomed to family members being around at all times.

After Raine returned thanks, they helped their plates and Jessie realized just how hungry she was. As they ate their meal, she heard the little goldfinch in the background singing his heart out.

"Tell me about the goldfinch you have in the cage."

"Oh, Timo?" Raine grinned, "My grandmother was driving down the road one day this past year and he literally fell out of the sky right in front of her. She didn't really know what it was at first. It looked like a falling leaf but was too heavy for that so she turned around and came back. This little bird was sitting just on the edge of the pavement and at first glance, Grandma thought it had broken its neck. He was totally unaware when she scooped him up and put him in the truck. Something would surely have gotten him if she had left him there and she could not stand to think of that. When she got him home, she realized that he had injured his wing, as well, but he started becoming aware of his surroundings and eventually she realized his neck had not been broken after all. She thought to keep him a few days and nurse him back to health, but his wing just hung down more and more. She tried to tape it up, but it was simply broken too badly for those efforts. So she made a cage out of her glass atrium, named him 'Timo' and he has lived here since."

"Well, he certainly seems happy," Jessie observed.

"He sings all the time and Grandma just adores him. Of course, she would have been happier if she could have fixed his wing, but he has surely lived longer than he would have otherwise. And, she spoils him dreadfully."

"Well, I think he is adorable, so it would be hard not to spoil him."

Jessie turned her attention from the beautiful little bird and his happy birdsong to the table laden with food. At Raine's insistence, she helped herself to an additional serving.

"You are going to have me gaining weight before our wedding at this rate!" She complained good-naturedly.

"With all that you do, I don't think that will be a problem," Raine replied as he looked at her with admiration.

"Remember that I have not been hiking lately. Ceasing that strenuous exercise could change things for me."

"Well, it hasn't so far. You are beautiful as always," Raine, with love shining from his eyes, reached to hold her hand once again, then released it so that she could finish her meal.

Hearing the sound of a motor, Raine jumped up and headed to the door, motioning for Jessie to remain quiet. To his great relief, he saw his grandma driving up in the car, Uncle Charlie sitting in the passenger's seat.

Jessie, breathing a sigh of relief, arose to get a couple more place settings as her uncle and Raine's grandmother gained the door.

Both smiled broadly at Jessie and then looked at the table with gratitude. They seemed hungry and Jessie took that as a good sign. She noted fleetingly that Uncle Charlie seemed to have more color in his cheeks. He certainly still looked painfully thin but she knew staying here would change that.

Grandma headed across the floor to Jessie with outstretched arms.

"Congratulations my dear. I am delighted that you have agreed to marry my handsome grandson!"

Jessie smiled with delight as Grandma hugged her affectionately.

"Thank you, Mrs. Roberts," Jessie responded, blushing furiously.

"Nonsense! No 'Mrs. Roberts' for you. You may call me 'Nattie' or 'Grandma', whichever is most comfortable for you," Grandma, her eyes twinkling, held Jessie at arm's length.

"I am glad to see your beautiful hair has been set free today. I'm sure my grandson will agree. I'm sorry I was not here to set everything out for you, but it would seem that you two did just fine on your own."

Uncle Charlie came forward at this point and added his congratulations to the couple and shook hands with Raine and Jessie alike.

"Charlie, please get washed up and let's sit down to dinner. Getting up so early has made me ravenous!"

Charlie obediently did her bidding and then returned to what had already become 'his' place at the table. He sat down as Grandma passed each dish of the feast in his direction.

Raine and Jessie, though still finishing their own meals, were anxious to hear news about Jessie's grandpa, but they waited patiently until their older relatives were ready to divulge what they had learned.

"Have you two been able to reach any decisions about your plans?" asked Grandma as she bit into a chicken leg.

Raine swallowed and then replied for both of them, "We have discussed what we would like to have in a wedding and I think we have reached some agreements."

"Good. It is always best to hash everything out."

There was a pause and then Grandma looked Jessie's way and continued, "I am sure you are anxious to hear about your grandpa."

Jessie looked up in eagerness, "Yes, ma'am. Is he all right?"

"Well, if you are meaning his health, he has lost weight, but he seems to be all right otherwise. Spiritually, he is stronger than ever. He certainly has great faith. He had a private message to convey so he signed this," and Grandma worked her fingers trying to copy the sign that Grandpa had made.

"That means that he misses us terribly," Jessie interpreted with tears in her eyes.

Nattie reached over and placed a caring hand on top of Jessie's, "Child, I am so sorry that your grandpa is separated from you and your family. I know you were all close and it grieves me that you are apart, but we are working to get him released and hopefully it will be soon. Certainly by the time you get married."

A tear started making its way down Jessie's cheek and she brushed it away quickly, "Mrs... I mean Grandma Nattie, do you mind if I call you that?"

"Certainly not, I like the sound of it!"

"Well, Grandma Nattie, we have so much to thank you for . . . you have been so generous with our family and the way you are working to free Grandpa. The fact that you are learning sign language so that you can communicate with him secretly. There is just so much . . . I hardly know where to begin to thank you," Jessie stated with great earnestness in her eyes.

"Jessie, you don't need to thank me. We are almost family, you know, and I really have felt like we were family from the first time we met. That's what family do for one another, as you well know. You have demonstrated sacrificial love yourself for years. Let's just keep on loving like that. After all, that is what Jesus did for us, isn't it?"

"Yes, ma'am! There is no denying that!"

"Well, since that is settled I guess you will want to know what the lawyer said."

At that point Nattie looked at Uncle Charlie who took the floor, "The lawyer has been trying to get the bail reduced, but so far that hasn't happened. The bail is too high for us to raise short of selling the mountain."

"Oh, Uncle Charlie, you can't do that!" Jessie exclaimed, her eyes wide.

"Well, not at the moment, but we might want to consider that for the future. Apparently, there has been some interest in my property since the auction was advertised."

Jessie really looked alarmed now and that was not lost on anyone present.

"Jessie, if you and Raine get married and start adoption proceedings, the kids can finally come down off the mountain and I think it is apparent that I need to be in a more accessible place. What do I need the mountain for any more except for a place to hide you kids? Besides, Nattie has offered me their bunk house and I am seriously considering renting it from her."

"Now, Charlie, you know you can stay there all you want and I won't charge you a penny," Nattie interjected.

"Nattie, I won't consider staying without paying for it. Charlie McAlister always pays his way!" Uncle Charlie said firmly.

"Well, we can discuss that later, but I do think something can be worked out so its settled that you will be staying in the bunkhouse!" Nattie stated just as firmly.

A knot had started forming in Jessie's stomach. Things were moving along too rapidly for her tastes. She much preferred her answers coming directly from God.

Raine, noticing the change in Jessie, intervened. "I think we can all agree that Uncle Charlie will be staying in the bunkhouse," he smiled his infectious smile at them all.

"Plus, when Jessie and I are married we can take my room," Raine ducked his head at this statement and a crimson flush began making its way up the back of his neck but he cleared his throat and continued, "that will leave the guest bedroom for the three girls. It is big enough to put another small bed in there so that should work. And, if Charlie doesn't mind, the four boys can bunk with him. Also, when Grandpa gets out there is room for him to bunk there, too, if he would like."

"I would really hate to see you sell your property, Charlie, but it does belong to you and it is your decision, after all," Raine continued sympathetically.

Silence ensued in the room as each one present considered what Raine was saying. Jessie saw the wisdom in his words and could not argue with them. Even though she loved the mountain and would like for her uncle to keep it, she realized that she did not have any say so in that matter at all. It truly was his decision.

"Well, I am not going to go right out and sell it, but I recognize an opportunity is available that I should seriously consider. I'm not going to jeopardize the kids' welfare, however, opportunity or no!" Uncle Charlie said vehemently.

Jessie relaxed some with these words and thought that their life would be changing dramatically in the near future one way or another with her upcoming marriage.

"As far as the boys bunking with me is concerned, I ain't used to kids, but I think it's time I got to know my family anyway. That might be kinda nice. And, me and Kevin, of course, grew up together. We tolerated each other's quirks back then and we can do it again, I'm thinking."

Smiling at that, Jessie suddenly realized that her family was about to grow again by leaps and bounds. That caused fresh new love to swell up in her heart. It might be really nice after all and it would be so wonderful having Grandpa back again! Of course, the boys would love living in the bunkhouse and helping out around the farm. Her heart squeezed with pain, however, at the thought of never seeing the little cabin again or the beauty of the waterfall and view. She had truly not realized how much she had grown to love their home on Castleknob until now.

CHAPTER TWENTY-THREE

RAINE AND JESSIE visited some more with Grandma and Uncle Charlie, but no further decisions were made. Jessie offered to clean the kitchen, but Grandma Nattie shooed her out the door. She was instructed to spend some time with Raine. Grandma knew they had precious little of that and she wanted them getting better acquainted before their special day.

Shying away from being out in the open, Raine ushered Jessie into the barn. The dust motes hung heavy in the sunbeams that made their way through any opening, but the smell of fresh hay was sweet.

Dragging a hay bale over for Jessie to sit on, Raine stood and watched Thunder and Lacey in the corral. Jessie stuffed a stray lock of hair under her slouch hat, which she had donned again, and pulled her coat tighter around her. The fall day, though sunny, was proving to be on the cool side.

Not missing anything, Raine sat down beside Jessie and pulled her close. He intended to keep her warm if at all possible.

"I am sorry you had to hear about the probability of your uncle selling Castleknob. I know that must be a scary proposition for you," Raine said sympathetically, "especially since you have worked so hard to save it."

"God has been providing every step of the way, Raine, I cannot deny that, but we have grown to love it on that old mountain and it has certainly been a safe haven for us for so long now that to think of leaving that 'nest' is a little frightening," Jessie admitted honestly.

"Is marrying me a frightening proposition, as well?" Raine asked softly.

"Oh, Raine, everything is frightening right now, but marrying you is something I want with all of my heart!"

Smiling with pure pleasure, Raine tilted his head in that way that Jessie had so come to love and looked down at her, "I am more glad to hear that than you will ever know. I truly think that you will love living here on the farm. It is hard work, but enormously satisfying. I think your brothers and sisters will fit right in and we can get them enrolled in school eventually and all that that entails."

"Sarah and I have been schooling the younger ones, but I know they need to be around children their own age. They don't seem to miss that now, but eventually they will, I'm thinking."

Raine just looked at her with great affection as she continued, "I believe the sleeping arrangements that you have determined will work well and, of course, the children will be excited to live on a farm and be back with Grandpa again. We have missed him so much!"

"I know you have, Jessie. We just need to get you back together again as soon as possible."

Suddenly Jessie clung to Raine, "I am so frightened to bring the children off the mountain. What if something goes wrong with our plans and they are taken away. I could not bear to live with that after my promise to mother!"

"Jessie, we will do nothing until I have talked to a lawyer and made certain of the outcome. I do want to marry you as soon as possible, but I am willing to wait until the timing is right. In no wise will we jeopardize your family," Raine replied with sincerity.

Breathing a deep sigh of relief, Jessie relaxed against Raine. How she loved this man! She knew instinctively she could trust him. She just needed to place this all in God's hands and continue to trust Him, too, as He worked this plan out through Raine.

CHAPTER TWENTY-FOUR

SARAH BUSTLED AROUND the kitchen cleaning up after their meal. She had noticed that Jessie seemed unusually quiet since Raine had brought her home. Her mind was busy with conjecturing just what could be wrong. She hoped they had not had a lover's quarrel. She knew in her heart that Raine was the right man for her oldest sister and she did not want anything interfering with that.

Jessie helped with the children's baths with little being said. Now that Sarah had thought some more about it, Jessie seemed downright sad. Not the emotion she was expecting from a bride-to-be.

The evening seemed to drag, and Sarah was grateful when all of the little ones had been put to bed and she could finally ask Jessie in the privacy of their bedroom just what was going on.

Crawling into bed beside the now sleeping Katy and Annie, Sarah reached over and tapped Jessie on the arm in order to gain her attention. She signed her concern and asked Jessie whatever could be wrong.

Jessie glanced down to ensure that Katy was truly asleep. Deciding not to risk anything, however, she signed rather than voiced her concerns to Sarah.

Sarah's eyes flew open wide. She studied the rough wall of their bedroom as she considered just what Jessie's message meant.

Uncle Charlie was considering selling the mountain! Fear gripped its roughened fingers around Sarah's heart and squeezed tight. No one, not even Jessie understood just how much Sarah loved this mountain. Everyone loved her here. There was no one to make fun of her disability or grab her as her uncle had done when she had not been able to scream her terror. Sarah paled at the thought of leaving her sanctuary.

Jessie noted the change in Sarah's color and immediately sought to reassure her.

She sat up in bed and leaned over to whisper her words in Sarah's ears.

"Sarah, this mountain belongs to Uncle Charlie. We really have no right to interfere with his plans for it. We don't have enough money for taxes to save it so we couldn't even try to pay him rent. I am sick about it myself, but what can we do? We are staying here on his good graces right now. He could have kicked us out if he had wanted to! Besides, you will like it on the farm. It is lovely there and when Grandpa is out of jail and everything is settled, you will be able to go to town and shop for yourself. The children will be enrolled in school and will be able to make new friends..."

Jessie stopped her flow of words as she realized that the more she said the more upset Sarah seemed to be getting.

"Sarah, talk to me. Tell me what is going on in that beautiful head of yours."

Sarah simply shook her head, however, and signed, "I want you to be happy right now Jessie. You have a right to be. You will soon be a new bride. Brides should be happy!"

"Believe me, Sarah, I am deliriously happy about that! It's just that this mountain had become our home. It has sheltered us and protected us and we have delighted daily in its beauty. Maybe God is saying that now it is time we move on to the next phase of our lives."

Turning to look her sister full in the face she noted that Sarah still did not look any happier.

"Is something else wrong, Sarah?" Jessie asked gently.

Sarah hung her head and signed that she did not want to talk about this anymore.

After a pause, she turned back to Jessie and signed, "You haven't told Micah yet, have you?"

Jessie took a deep breath, "No . . . I will get him aside tomorrow and tell him then."

Turning once more and signing to Jessie, "I will pray for you," Sarah scooted down in the bed and faced the wall.

Sighing again, Jessie blew out the lamp, positioned herself under the covers and prepared to face a sleepless night.

. . . .

The next morning after breakfast, Jessie followed Micah out to the barn. When they were out of earshot of Josh, Jessie prayed for courage and then began.

"Micah, I need to speak to you about something."

After a moment, Micah, who was sharpening his axe for his woodcutting, turned to say, "I could tell something was up, Jessie. What is it?"

Without preamble, Jessie began, "Uncle Charlie has someone interested in his property. He is seriously considering selling."

Micah paused in his work and then turned slowly to face his sister, "Well, I wasn't expecting that! How do you feel about this?"

"Honestly, it makes me feel sick, but what are we to do? If he decides to sell, we don't have a leg to stand on."

"Does Raine know about this?"

"Yes, it was discussed over lunch yesterday. He offered a solution that when he and I are married, all of us can come to live at the farm, including Grandpa when he is released."

Micah did not immediately respond. He looked up at the rafters in the old barn and then watched a piece of straw as it fell through the cracks and then landed on the rough ground, which was the floor of the barn.

Jessie was beginning to think that Micah was not going to respond at all when he turned and studied her intently. He brushed a work-roughened hand across his blond hair as its length was beginning to get into his eyes. Jessie thought absent-mindedly that it was time for Sarah to give him another haircut.

Finally, Micah breathed deeply and stated softly, "I think we have all grown to love this place. It has been home for over two years now. It is the only place Annie has ever known," Micah paused again reflectively, "It has certainly been hard on you living here, what with all the trips off the mountain and the pressure of trying to keep up with the demand for food for all of us growing kids," he grinned at her affectionately, then sobered.

"We have all learned to trust God here. And, we have been happier than I could ever have imagined without Mom and Dad. Sarah has become quite a cook and you have wood skills that would make you the envy of any man. We have all worked together, even the little ones. As a result, we are all healthy and strong. I sometimes think that separation from the world has given us each unique qualities. But there are good things about living in a community, too. I do remember that much."

Jessie turned and looked towards where Josh was working, still just out of earshot. She sighed deeply and then turned once more to face her eldest brother.

"Micah, I would feel guilty about this if it just involved my upcoming marriage," Jessie began only to be interrupted by Micah.

"Jess, you cannot help what has happened regarding Uncle Charlie's property. You, certainly more than anyone else, have worked hard to save this place! The auction just served to attract attention to one of the most beautiful places on this earth!"

"Thanks, Micah, and you are probably right about the auction attracting the potential buyer."

"Nevertheless, I would hate to leave here."

"I feel the same way, too, but we have to consider Uncle Charlie and Grandpa. Uncle Charlie needs the money from his place to pay for his expenses since he can't really work anymore or live here easily. Grandpa could possibly be bailed out of jail until all of this mess can be worked out, too"

"Jessie, Uncle Charlie could simply come back to his own cabin and we could do the work for him since that is what we have been doing all along."

"But what about medical needs and doctor visits?"

"We could work that out. They wouldn't be taking place every day would they?"

"Well, no . . ."

"The thing is, Jessie, I just don't believe it is time to leave this mountain. Let things be worked out a little more before we do that. We are risking fulfilling Mama's last wish if we move too quickly."

Jessie stared at her brother with her heart in her throat. In spite of her resolve to trust Raine and God, Micah was giving voice to her deep-seated concerns.

The baby goat bleated in the distance as Josh took a break and started playing with it. Both Jessie and Micah watched as it's mama came running to check things out.

Jessie smiled and Micah laughed out loud.

"There is also the issue of Raine and his grandma," Micah continued, "Just how much trouble would they be in if the authorities found out they have known about us for a little while now and have even been keeping us supplied with food. They are even considering harboring us if we move down there?"

"I have thought about all of that, too. Raine assures me it will be all right, but I don't want to risk it," Jessie responded honestly.

"Of course, we could go off the mountain and turn ourselves in and get Grandpa off the hook. But would he want that? He certainly has made no effort to do that for himself so I think we should follow his lead there."

"I think you are right, Micah. Grandpa has sacrificed his freedom all this time to keep us together so it does seem right that we should follow his wisdom and example."

"Let's pray about it and wait and see what happens, Jess," Micah said as he turned towards her once more, "Who knows, Uncle Charlie may decide not to sell or maybe the buyers will decide they don't want it anymore. Let's just sit tight for right now and wait on the Lord's leading."

Jessie suddenly smiled a brilliant smile, visible even in the low light of the barn's interior, "I knew I could count on you to set me straight. You have learned a lot under Grandpa's tutelage," Jessie reached and hugged her brother affectionately as she spoke.

Micah smiled his thanks and asked, "When will you see Raine next?"

"He is supposed to be back up tomorrow."

"Then why don't you just be happy as you are waiting to see him again," Micah asked as he turned to exit the barn and go on about his chores.

"I think I can handle that assignment!" Jessie laughed as she took her leave of her brother.

CHAPTER TWENTY-FIVE

REINING IN HER feelings as best she could, Jessie awaited Raine's arrival. She had to admit, she would be glad to get off the mountain. Micah had seemed to take everything in stride since their talk. Sarah, however, was another story. She was not communicating much at present and even though she was always quiet, of course, the silence right now was deafening. She went about her chores as usual, but with a somber demeanor.

Jessie was truly worried about her, but could not get her to open up. Even the little ones had tried to liven her up but to no avail.

The sudden tap on the door served to make Jessie jump. She had truly been lost in thought. The twins jumped down from the bench at the table and ran to open the door before she could recover sufficiently.

Raine grinned broadly as he entered amidst a sea of giggles. It only took a split-second to realize that Jessie was not her usual happy self, however. He smiled again and attempted to enliven the somber mood in the cabin. Whatever had happened to cast such a pall over this happy family?

Jessie greeted Raine and then walked to the kitchen to strap on her backpack. In the meantime, Raine relieved himself of the supplies he had brought as he placed the packs on the trestle table. Sarah's eyes opened wide with gratitude.

Amongst the bags of flour, sugar and cornmeal was a small box of peppermint sticks. In another bag, carefully wrapped, were two more frozen beef roasts.

The little ones assailed Raine as this point and he was having a wonderful time rough-housing with the twins. They had not stopped giggling.

Stopping to hug Sarah, Jessie whispered in her ear, "Everything will work out just fine. You wait and see!"

Sarah attempted a smile and then signed her farewell to Raine and Jessie as they made their way out the front door.

They had only gone a few feet, however, when the door opened again and two little boys called out in unison, "Good-bye, Mr. Bo."

Jessie laughed for the first time and then grinned lovingly at Raine, "Looks like you may have a moniker that sticks for a while."

"That's all right with me as long as I am your 'Mr. Bo'," Raine replied as he reached for her hand to walk under the waterfall by her side.

The two spoke softly as they walked through the tunnel, but the issue hanging like a cloud over Jessie was not mentioned.

As was their habit now, neither spoke a word as they traveled down the mountain. Jessie delighted in the trip, however. The air was so crisp and cool and the fall odors were a delight to her senses. They approached the farmhouse at length and Jessie noted that the car was gone.

They were already in the warmth of the kitchen with Jessie inhaling the aroma of freshly baked donuts before Raine ventured to say anything.

"Grandma got up early again so that she could fry up a big platter of doughnuts for everyone before she and

Charlie left. So, let's sit down and eat our share and not disappoint her."

"I must admit the fall air has revved up my appetite," Jessie declared as she took the seat that Raine pulled out for her at the table.

"Go ahead and get some while I pour us some coffee," Raine offered graciously.

"I think I can wait long enough for the blessing," Jessie laughingly replied.

She did not have to wait long, however, and was sinking her teeth into the soft, glazed surface before she knew it. Between the two of them they must have devoured a dozen before they came up for air.

"Boy, are these good!" Jessie declared as she gingerly licked her sugary fingers.

"I'll be sure to tell Grandma that you thought they were finger-licking good!" Raine exclaimed as Jessie punched him playfully on the arm.

"I've got to wash up before I get this stickiness everywhere," Jessie responded.

"All right, now that we are full and out of earshot of everyone please tell me what was wrong at the cabin," Raine asked as he grew serious upon her return.

"Oh, Raine, even with your generous offer of a place to live for my family, it was still difficult telling Sarah and Micah that Uncle Charlie is considering selling his property."

"I can well understand that. I am sure you have felt secure in your seclusion there and the thought of leaving that security must be hard for you," Raine stated sympathetically.

"I was pleased at how Micah took the news. He was surprised, but his attitude was to wait and see. He approached this potential change with faith. It was really refreshing!"

"And, how did Sarah take it?"

"She was the real surprise. She was shocked, of course, but then it distressed her and I could not talk her out of it. As a matter of fact, the more I talked about it and tried to reason with her, the more upset she became. And, now she has just closed up," Jessie confessed with tears in her eyes.

Raine reached to take her hand, "Hmm, do you know what that is all about?"

"No," Jessie replied honestly.

"Sarah has never been strong or accepted change very well. She has certainly blossomed on the mountain, however, and is now the picture of health and strength. She has thrived in that environment more than any of the rest of us. It really suits her. But I just do not have an answer for your question. I am not exactly sure what is wrong. At least, I thought she would open up to me about it, but that has not happened so far."

"Well, we are talking about a major change in your lives and it has to be a scary thought for all of you. Maybe when Grandma and Charlie return they will have good news about your grandpa and you can take her something positive today."

"So that is where your grandma and Uncle Charlie have gone. Back to see Grandpa?"

"Actually, the lawyer's office called late yesterday afternoon and asked them if they could come first thing this morning. They left early to be there when he opened. We are all hoping for something good to come of this," Raine finished with an enthusiasm he did not fully feel.

Jessie's stomach tightened up considerably at this news. She felt uneasy, but determined to be optimistic about the outcome of today's meeting.

Raine had chores that had to be done so Jessie went to the barn with him. They had agreed not to talk until they were back in the safety of the house so both worked side by side silently.

Thinking how wonderful it was to be working by Raine's side, Jessie thought about their future and that it would be hard but very fulfilling living on a farm. It was obvious that Raine loved what he was doing and was well-suited to the work with his muscular frame.

They were working so hard that they did not immediately hear the vehicle approaching. Raine grasped Jessie by the shoulders and gently pushed her into a corner behind hay bales before he sauntered out of the barn. Blessedly, it was a false alarm, however, as Grandma parked the car and moved to the far side to help Charlie out.

Raine noted their expressions before he spoke and knew instinctively that the news was not good. He glanced around to make sure all was clear and returned to the barn to get Jessie and bring her inside.

As they entered the kitchen, Jessie willed herself to be calm. Something was terribly wrong.

Grandma indicated that they should all take a seat at the table and discuss what they had been told by the lawyer.

Getting right to the point, Grandma began, "The lawyer called us to his office today because he wanted to let us know that efforts were going to be stepped up to find your family, Jessie."

She paused and gauged Jessie's reaction, "The authorities have really been interrogating your grandfather unmercifully. He looked really bad today. They are starting to say that perhaps he did more than kidnap you kids."

At this news, Jessie gasped and put her hand over her mouth.

"They are even starting to suspect Charlie with having something to do with your disappearance as the date he left the mountain and the time you left your home are only a few months apart. They have sent someone down to Ninety Six to interrogate the hospital and nursing home staff just to make sure Charlie's story checks out."

Tears came to Jessie's eyes at this news and she reached to lay her hand on Uncle Charlie's arm.

"Raine, you need to take Jessie home immediately and, Jessie, unfortunately you need to stay there until further notice. Tell me what all you need in the way of supplies right now and I will try to fix you up out of my pantry."

Grandma rose to get the items Jessie said they needed and Raine went to saddle Thunder.

Charlie looked at Jessie with sorrow in his eyes and continued, "Jessie, your grandpa is tough, but I honestly don't know how much more of this he can take. They have really stepped things up now. I'm convinced that your uncle Sean is behind all of this. He has a real vendetta against Kevin and he seems to be enjoying watching this unfold. Nattie and I both think he has been lying about Kevin and has stirred up all of this new furor."

"I think maybe it's time I made a trip down myself and told the truth about us," Jessie began only to be interrupted by her uncle.

Jessie began only to be interrupted by her uncle.

"You need to know, Jessie, that when you do that the authorities will demand that you bring the rest of your family in to prove your words. At that point, your brothers and sisters will be placed in protective custody, divided up and put in foster homes. Sean has indicated once again that he will take you and Sarah. He don't know that you have turned eighteen yet so he would in all likelihood end up with just Sarah and that will be over my dead body," Uncle Charlie finished with fire darting out of his eyes.

Jessie visibly paled at that thought.

"Uncle Charlie, I need to go back to the mountain and pray this through. There has to be a reasonable solution. There just has to be!"

Grandma called from the pantry and asked Jessie to assist her in carrying the bags out to the barn. Once there, they were hurriedly stuffed into the saddle bags and Grandma turned to hug Jessie and apologize for sending her off hungry.

By that time Uncle Charlie had made his way to the barn and Jessie hugged him carefully and tried to assure him that it would all work out. She saw the huge doubt looming in his eyes, however, and that alone caused tears to stream down her cheeks.

"Raine, please get her home as fast as you can and get back here yourself. I am afraid we may get a visit any moment. Please be careful!" Grandma urged as she grasped Raine's arm.

As it was, Raine and Jessie were barely out of sight on the shortcut, when they heard a vehicle going down Raine's driveway and peering cautiously through the trees saw it was the Sheriff's car.

Raine urged Thunder on unmercifully as they ascended the rough trail to Castleknob. Jessie clung tightly to Raine's chest, but still it was difficult to hang on. She had never been so terrified in all her life. All the ones she loved most were in terrible danger, except for her father, and who knows maybe he was in danger, too.

The whole way up the mountain, Jessie prayed fervently. Her first prayers were for Nattie and Uncle Charlie that God would protect them and give them wisdom in their answers. Then she prayed for herself and Raine that they would not be detected and that she could reach her siblings and warn them of this imminent danger.

And what about Raine reaching the farm again without raising any suspicions? Her heart thumped wildly against his back as she considered all of the implications involved. Surely God would protect them. He had certainly brought them this far. She just had to believe He would see them through this thing, too. Had He not been faithful in the past?

In one way the trip seemed to take forever and in another it was over before she knew it. She might not see Raine again for some time. She was filled with grief at the thought.

Carefully scouting the area, Raine decided to ride Thunder up on the boulders until they were almost at the cave entrance. He dismounted quickly and assisted Jessie. Then moving rapidly, he unstrapped the packs and being ever vigilant, he and Jessie moved behind the boulder and short trees until they were safely inside the cave.

Jessie insisted that they unpack the supplies just inside the tunnel. She and the boys would return and retrieve the items after Raine had left. She turned to face Raine after lighting the torch.

Even with the fright written on her face, Raine thought she had never looked more lovely. His heart breaking, he hugged her close, "Jessie, you know I love you and I will be doing everything in my power to work things out for you. I don't know when I will be back, but I will come to your door when I think it is safe. Please, promise me you will not leave the cabin for any reason."

"I promise . . . at least as much as it is in my power to keep such a promise," Jessie murmured

"Fair enough. I've got to go, but stay safe," Raine brushed her lips with a tender kiss and then was gone.

CHAPTER TWENTY-SIX

SARAH KNEW WHEN Jessie entered the cabin that something was terribly wrong. When Jessie gathered the family together immediately and told the children that they would be playing the "quiet" game again, Sarah paled at the meaning of this news alone.

"Micah, I will need you and Josh to help me retrieve the supplies that Raine brought up the mountain for us," Jessie simply turned and headed back out the door as she uttered this request and her brothers followed.

When they entered the tunnel, Micah asked quietly, "Jess, what is this all about."

Turning with a stricken look, Jessie briefly told him the latest news. Micah shook his head as he looked at the floor of the tunnel. Then he looked Jessie directly in the eyes, "Remember, we have been here before without any outside help and God has brought us safely through."

Had she not been holding the torch, Jessie would have hugged her brother at those words! When would she ever learn not to falter in her faith?

The trio gathered the packages without incident and delivered them to the kitchen.

Sarah's eyes brightened at the sight of all the supplies which Grandma Nattie had sent. Jessie explained that these items were directly from Raine's grandmother's pantry. They would replace them later though she was sure that Grandma Nattie would protest.

Then Jessie asked Josh to take the little ones to the girl's bedroom and play quietly there while she, Micah and Sarah had a family conference.

"The sheriff's car was driving up as Raine and I entered the shortcut today on the way home," Jessie began. "If we had been delayed by even a minute he would have seen us."

Sarah shuddered involuntarily.

Jessie reached and patted Sarah's hand and then continued, "Uncle Charlie believes that Sean is behind this new search effort. Grandpa will not be given custody of us kids now even if he is released. The authorities have made that clear."

Pausing as her words sunk in, Jessie looked at her brother and sister. Both looked greatly disturbed by this news but when she told them about Grandpa's state of mind and health and just what he was being accused of now, Sarah bowed her head and wept silent tears.

Micah looked miserable and suddenly jumped up from the table and crossed to look out the window.

Waiting until both had calmed down some, Jessie continued, "I am equally concerned for Uncle Charlie. He has been through so much already and he is being implicated, too, in our disappearance. They have gone to Ninety Six to check out his story."

Sarah looked back up at that point and signed quickly, "Are they going to arrest him, too?"

"I'm not sure what all is going to happen before this ends, Sarah," Jessie uttered softly.

Micah came back to the table. Looking down at his sisters, he uttered softly, "Maybe it's time we turn ourselves in . . ."

"I had the same thought, Micah, but Uncle Charlie does not share our sentiments," she paused and looked in Sarah's direction. Then continuing carefully, "All of you would be separated up into foster homes and lose all semblance of any kind of control over your own lives. Since I am already eighteen, I would be on my own. Uncle Charlie believes we should continue to stay hidden and let the adults fight our battle."

"What a mess! All we want to do is stay together and fulfill our own mother's dying wish and why can't anyone understand that! Why rip a family apart!" Micah gave way to his feelings and then sat back down at the table and spreading his hands out in front of him, took a deep breath.

"It's okay to vent, Micah," Jessie said softly, "Deep down we all feel the same way. Bottom line, however, should always be that we continue trusting God. After all, as you said earlier, He has brought us this far."

Micah's smile in response to her statement was tight, but he took another deep breath and attempted to calm himself down.

Jessie gazed upon her two siblings with the intense affection she felt for them and broached the one thing that she could think of that might work. "I believe Raine is cautiously consulting with his lawyer about he and I adopting the rest of you when we are married. Personally, I believe that is the only thing that might work other than staying hidden here until all of us are grown, if that were possible."

Jessie's attempt to lighten the mood only evoked half-hearted smiles so she continued, "Of course, God's ways are not our ways and He might have something entirely different in mind. At present, we just need to wait and see."

Sarah arose at this statement and signed slowly, "In the meantime, we have a hungry family to feed so I will finish our meal."

Micah only lingered a moment longer and then turned to Jessie, "I need to get on with my chores. I'll listen out for any different sounds but I'm praying it will just be another beautiful day on the mountain. I'll leave King Wolf indoors but I will come back later with a rope and we can walk him."

With that Micah patted Wolf on the head and left.

Jessie headed for the bedroom to check on the little ones and Josh and then decided to spend some time alone in prayer before she returned to help take care of her family.

CHAPTER TWENTY-SEVEN

THE NEXT FEW days passed with no news from Raine. Jessie realized that Uncle Charlie's deadline for the payment of his taxes was fast approaching. Even if the authorities failed to find them hidden as they were, there was the real danger of a new owner finding them eventually.

Jessie prayed continually. She looked at each precious family member throughout the day and faced the reality that someone else could be raising these children soon. Then a determination rose up inside her and a strength she knew was beyond herself pervaded her being. God designed the family unit. He intended that little children be raised in that loving environment. If they did not have each other and were left alone, she could see being taken into another family unit and raised there. But they DID have each other. She knew with her entire being that God intended for this family to remain together. They had a love for one another that only God could have sown in their hearts.

Scriptures flooded Jessie's mind and with them came the faith in God that she so desperately sought. She had never felt so strong in her faith before and she KNEW that God had worked everything out.

Just as strong was the prodding that it was time to go off the mountain. Jessie immediately arose and began her preparations. She accepted the fact that Micah and Sarah would protest but she could not shake the feeling that it was what she was to do.

As it turned out, both siblings were in the barn so she simply told Josh she would be back later and walked out the door.

She was ramrod straight in her purpose and felt as if there were angels at her back prodding her on.

Descending the mountain had never felt so good and Jessie's legs were as frisky as young pups. Not a moment's fear assailed her as she turned off onto the shortcut to Raine's house.

The car was not there but she could hear Raine in the barn talking soothingly to one of his horses. She ventured forth cautiously not wanting to startle him, but the horse had already signaled her approach.

Raine's eyes grew big when he saw her, but he simply whispered, "Jessie."

Then he came towards her and took her immediately in his arms.

"What are you doing here? Is everyone all right?"

"Yes, we are fine."

Raine glanced around cautiously, "You could have been seen."

"I know, but I believe God will protect me. I really felt an urgency to get off the mountain today. I don't understand it myself, but it was as if an angel was behind me spurring me on and protecting me along the way. I have really never felt anything like it before."

Jessie stopped and looked at Raine. He saw the wonder in her eyes and simply embraced her again. He longed to protect her, but he knew this particular danger to Jessie and her family would require God, himself. He would do his part, however, as long as he could.

A gentle neigh interrupted the moment and Jessie looked around Raine to see Lacey standing over a new little foal.

"Oh, Raine! Lacey had her baby!"

Chuckling softly at Jessie's excitement, Raine explained. "Yes, I have been up all night overseeing this delivery."

"So that is why you look so tired," Jessie whispered compassionately.

"I have known for several days that the time was approaching," Raine said.

"I couldn't have gone to see you no matter how badly I wanted to. This delivery was a very difficult one and I had to hang close by," Raine offered by way of explanation.

Jessie leaned into Raine placing her arm around his waist as she viewed this wobbly little one.

"I believe she was well worth the wait and work, however," Raine grinned, "see her markings?"

Nodding her head, Jessie looked back up at Raine.

"She's going to be a beaut! I would say my horse farm is off and running, pardon the pun."

Giggling softly, Jessie asked, "have you named her yet?"

"I have been too busy and now too tired to think of a name. Does something come to your mind?" Raine asked tentatively.

Before Jessie could answer, however, the sound of crunching gravel reached their ears.

"Quick, hide behind those hay bales while I check out who this is," Raine whispered urgently.

Jessie walked softly to do his bidding, and had hidden herself by the time the door of the vehicle slammed.

Exiting the barn, Raine beheld a stranger before him who somehow seemed vaguely familiar. He was quite thin and had graying hair that belied his age.

Approaching cautiously, Raine asked affably, in an attempt to cover his nerves, "Can I help you?"

"I am hoping that you will be able to. At least, that is what I have been told in confidence. You are Raine Roberts?"

Raine hesitated, but before he could answer or ascertain the identity of the man, he heard running feet behind him. He glanced over his shoulder and to his great consternation, beheld Jessie quickly attaining his side. What was she thinking to come tearing out of the barn like that?

Jessie grabbed Raine's arm as if to steady herself and then dropped a bombshell with one word!

"Dad?"

When the man did not immediately respond, Jessie slowly removed her hat and let her long tresses loose. The sudden recognition in the man's eyes told the story. Extending his arms, Jessie ran into them.

Both father and daughter sobbed uncontrollably as they hugged each other tightly and a misty-eyed Raine looked on. They kept hugging and then holding one another at arm's length to look into each other's eyes, as if they really could not believe what they were seeing.

When at length Jessie could contain herself, she turned to Raine and formally introduced her father.

Extending his hand, Raine grasped the hand of his future father-in-law as the realization of just what this arrival meant dawned on him.

Turning to Jessie, Raine was mesmerized by the glow coming from her eyes. It took a moment before he could speak, but then coming to himself he offered graciously,

"Jessie, I believe this calls for a celebration. Let's go inside and spread out the meal Grandma prepared before she left. Looks like your dad could do with some of my Grandma's cooking. Besides, I'm as hungry as a bear myself."

Grinning from ear to ear, Jessie slipped her hand into the crook of her dad's arm and led him along to the kitchen. Once inside, Raine showed Mr. McKaine where he could wash up and then did so himself while Jessie placed on the table the feast that she had come to understand was commonplace.

Seated between the two men, Jessie reached to grasp the hand of each one as Raine bowed his head for the blessing.

"Father..." Raine's voice broke temporarily, but he took a deep breath and continued, "Father, we stand in awe of the miracle you have performed in bringing Jessie's father back to his family. What an awesome God you are to supply just what we needed right when it was needed the most! We praise your name for this enormous blessing and the blessing of this meal. Bless my grandmother who prepared it and bless it to the nourishment of our bodies. May we use the strength you give us from it for your honor and glory. It is in the name of your Son, Jesus, that we pray. Amen."

Pure joy shone from Jessie's eyes as she glanced at Raine in appreciation of this special blessing. She noted that her father was too choked up from it to speak at present.

Raine began passing the bowls of food to Jessie's father who did not hesitate to fill his plate. Jessie watched as both men began to eat hungrily. She believed at this moment that she had never been so happy in all of her life!

There were so many questions running through Jessie's mind, but she knew Raine had been up all night with Lacey and her father was eating as if he had not eaten in years.

She pushed the questions from her mind for the moment and concentrated on her extreme pleasure to finally be with her father again.

Presently, with the need for hunger satisfied, Raine ventured a question himself, "If I can ask, how did you know to come here, Mr. McKaine?"

"Jessie's grandfather told me to," was the stunning answer that he received.

Jessie looked at her father with alarm, "Did anyone hear him?"

"No, as he signed the message to me when I went to see him."

"Is he all right?" Jessie asked tentatively.

"He looked bad, but when he realized who it was standing before him, he broke down in tears."

Jessie's father choked back his own emotions and then continued, "He knows his own ordeal will be over soon and that you kids will be taken care of now so that is what he needed to happen most,"

Looking her way, he continued, "I just have to present you children to the authorities and I believe we can clear this all up in short order."

Jessie's eyes spilled over with tears of gratitude at this news and it took a moment to contain herself before she could respond.

Raine offered Jessie's father another helping of food in order to allow Jessie enough time to compose herself, but he leaned back in his chair and declined graciously.

Looking at her father Jessie asked carefully, "Are you ready to take a trip up the mountain."

"As I recall it is a couple hours of hiking."

Raine interrupted at this point and offered Thunder for the ride up.

"I cannot leave Lacey and her new foal or I would come with you myself, but Thunder can cut considerable time off your trip. Besides, you will be wanting to get there as quickly as possible to see the rest of your family."

"Son, that is mighty nice of you and I believe I will take you up on your offer. I have waited a very long time to see my family again and even a few moments at this point that I can shave off the wait will be worth it," Jessie's father declared as he arose from the table and once again shook Raine's hand.

"I will just go saddle up and he will be ready in no time," Raine also rose and turned to go but called over his shoulder, "Jessie, Grandma has some grocery items packed up for you in the pantry. You can take those, too, when you leave."

Jessie began gathering up the bowls of food from the table and putting them away. Hearing the clatter of dishes, she realized that her father was helping clear the table, too.

"Dad, I can do this," she protested.

"We can get on our way more quickly if I help out," her father countered.

Not able to argue with that logic, Jessie continued her task with her beloved father at her side. How astonished everyone would be when she showed back up at the cabin with their father in tow!

CHAPTER TWENTY-EIGHT

IN NO TIME, the father and daughter were astride Thunder, the supplies in the saddle bags, making their way up the mountain.

With her arms clutched around her father, Jessie realized just how very thin he was. She choked back tears as she came to understand the suffering he had endured wherever he had been detained.

"So who exactly is this young man, Raine?" her father asked over his shoulder as Thunder's gait evened out in the one straight place on the trail.

"He is my fiancé," Jessie stated simply.

"I was impressed with him. He obviously cares a great deal for you and prayed quite a prayer!"

"Yes, he is growing in his walk," Jessie replied with enthusiasm.

Thunder lurched upward at this point, so father and daughter concentrated on the rigors of the trail until they attained Shelter Rock.

Upon reaching this stopping point, Jessie's dad dismounted and offered his hand to his daughter. Accepting same, she dismounted and Thunder was given a much needed rest. Looking off at the view and taking a deep breath, Jessie felt this was as good a time as ever, "Dad, do you know about Mom?" she asked softly.

When he did not answer her, Jessie grew concerned. She reached out her hand and rested it on his arm. Slowly, he turned and Jessie saw the tears streaming down his face.

"I knew in my heart some time ago that she was gone," he stated simply with a catch in his voice, "but, I was faced with the reality of it only a couple of days ago. I visited her gravesite before seeing her father." Pausing, Jessie's father allowed the tears to freely flow. "Finding him in jail accused of kidnapping my children was a difficult thing, indeed. I did not know what to believe until I realized that he was signing to me covertly. I have never been so relieved in all my life! To learn that you kids were safe meant the world to me."

"Did you receive Mom's letters?" Jessie asked tentatively.

"Only a short while ago," choking down a sob, he continued, "in one of them she told me she was pregnant again. She sounded so happy about it," Jessie's father's thin shoulders shook with his grief.

Putting her arm around her father, Jessie grieved with him.

"Did the baby survive?" he asked when finally, he could continue.

"Oh, Dad, you didn't know?" Jessie asked with contrition and then exclaimed softly, "She is a beautiful little girl!"

"Another little girl . . . I am blessed," he stated, his eyes shining.

"She will be overjoyed to meet you. She has heard so much about you! Her name is Annie."

"Annie . . . I like that . . ."

Looking off into the distance once more, McKaine took a deep breath and turned to remount Thunder. Grasping

Jessie's hand he helped her up and they continued on their way.

Reaching the field at last, Jessie told her dad they should dismount at the tree next to the spring and tie Thunder there.

Glancing around, her dad ventured, "I remember when we were here before that you and your grandpa tried to locate your uncle Charlie's cabin but only found him. Is the cabin close-by?"

Jessie just grinned radiantly and reached for her father's hand. She pulled him along partway up Castleknob. Then with her head, pointed down at the almost hidden opening. Her father looked at her quizzically and then noticed that Jessie was surveying the area carefully.

Realizing just what she was doing, Jessie confessed, "For almost three years we have kept our whereabouts a secret. It is very much a habit with me to make sure we are alone."

Then she extracted her flashlight from her backpack, carefully dropped into the hole and indicated that her dad was to do likewise. Once in the cave, her father let out a low whistle.

"Pretty neat, huh?" Jessie asked proudly, "We stayed here our first night on the mountain."

Then, keeping to the edge of the cave, Jessie led her father around to the small boulder.

"We have the twins and their curiosity to thank for discovering this," she stated simply as she knelt and pushed the boulder away from the opening.

Crawling through, Jessie lit the torch and reached for her father's hand to help him stand once inside.

She noted his incredulous look and then handed him the torch while she turned her flashlight off and knelt once again to pull the boulder back in place.

"We save a little of our battery this way," Jessie offered by way of explanation as she stood, "We have all learned to be very frugal in our time on this mountain. And, of course, the boulder has to be pulled back in place."

She took the torch once again and led her father through the tunnel to the massive door at its end. Hearing another low whistle, Jessie turned and grinned at him, "It gets even better than this."

She took out the old skeleton key and turned, then pulled back as the old lock, with a groan, submitted to its opening.

With assistance from her father, she grasped and then pulled on the timber door until, with much creaking, it swung wide to reveal its secret.

Her father stood surveying the backside of the waterfall with his mouth agape. Reaching once again for his hand, Jessie led him behind it until they were in view of the cabin.

"I would never have found you here, Jessie, if you had not been at the Robert's farm this morning. Raine could not have left his mare to bring me and I would have been at a loss."

"I know you are anxious to see everyone, so I will explain how this came about later. Just suffice it to say that God takes care of all the details, even seemingly small ones."

"Are you ready?" Jessie asked anxiously.

Taking a deep breath, her father faced the cabin and stated softly, "I have waited for this for way too long a time."

Approaching the door of the cabin, soft giggling could be heard coming from the other side. Jessie smiled at her father as he took another deep breath. Then she opened the door.

Standing to the side of her father, Jessie surveyed the scene in front of her. The little ones looked up from the floor where they were sitting surrounding Sarah who was standing in their midst. Sarah, whose back was to the door, saw the startled looks of the children and turned to see who had entered, thinking it to be one of the boys.

Katy, however, sprang to her feet with her rosebud mouth gaping open. Then she squealed and ran the short distance into her father's arms. He picked her up and swung her around as she grasped his neck tightly. "Oh, Daddy! You came for us. I knew you would!"

Jessie could see what must surely be a cry of joy coming from Sarah's lips as she still stood in the midst of her other siblings. Then she walked as if in slow motion across the floor to her beloved father. Seeing her coming towards him, her father gently placed Katy on the floor by his side and took Sarah in his arms. With tears of joy streaming down both faces, McKaine crooned into her ash-blond locks, "It's okay, Sarah, I'm home now."

Finally holding Sarah at arm's length, her dad planted a gentle kiss on her forehead and then placing his arm over her shoulder spied the twins who were standing in the middle of the floor now holding on to one another. Sarah stepped back and held her hand to her mouth as she continued to sob out her joy.

"Don't you remember me, boys?" their father asked with tears standing in his eyes.

Ryler looked at Tyler then and stated with excitement, "It really is our daddy!"

Then both boys ran in unison into their father's arms as he knelt on one knee to receive them.

Jessie moved across the room to kneel down beside Annie, who was looking confused and a little frightened. As the hugs and kisses dissipated between the twins and their father, Jessie lifted Annie into her arms and approached the others.

Standing up, McKaine looked with awe at the child he had never seen and then reached out his hand to touch Annie's soft curls, "My, Annie, how beautiful you are!"

Leaning back against Jessie shyly, she never-the-less looked at her dad with great interest, "Are you my daddy?"

"That I am little one," her father replied softly as tears streamed down his face. "Would you be willing to give your daddy his first hug from you?"

"I've been saving it for you, daddy," Annie responded in her matter-of-fact manner as she reached her chubby little arms to wrap them around his neck.

Everyone wept at this sight and then the ever rambunctious twins started a march around the living room stating loudly, "Daddy's home! Daddy's home!"

Suddenly the kitchen door opened and Micah entered quickly, "Quieten down, boys! I could hear you all the way to the barn!"

Then he stopped in mid-stride as he beheld the man still holding Annie standing in the midst of his brothers and sisters, "Dad?" he asked incredulously.

"This cannot be my son, Micah, can it?" their father asked as he stood gazing upon the young man in front of him.

"My word, he has become a man!"

Micah stepped through his siblings at this point and headed for his dad. Handing Annie back to Jessie, his father grasped him in a tight hug. Both father and son wept unashamedly as they held on for dear life.

Then holding one another at arm's length, they surveyed each other before engaging in another bear hug.

Finally, their father broke away and asked with some concern, "But, where is Josh?"

They heard soft scratching at the kitchen door at this point and it opened to reveal King Wolf on a rope followed by Josh. He dropped the rope and knelt to untie Wolf when he perceived that everyone was looking at him. He glanced around in confusion at the joy shining from the faces of his siblings and then beheld the man in their midst.

"Dad!" he yelled as he leapt to his feet and ran across the room.

Dropping down on one knee, McKaine hugged his son close. "My Josh, how tall you have gotten," he exclaimed.

Josh ducked his head as the tears streamed down his face and then rested it on his father's shoulder.

Wolf approached at this point and nuzzled Mr. McKaine. Dropping his hand from his son's back, he stroked the head of his children's pet and Wolf whined appropriately.

The twins started their merry cavorting again and Annie and Katy joined in. After years of trying to keep the children quiet during dangerous periods, Jessie felt the old urge to do so again. As she surveyed the joyous scene before her, however, it finally sunk in what their dad's presence truly meant.

They were in his care now and no one could take them away from him. It was over! The long wait was over! As their mother had requested, Jessie had kept the children together until their dad arrived. Her word to her mother had been fulfilled.

Such a wave of relief washed over Jessie that she responded physically to it. Noticing his eldest daughter weaving backwards, McKaine reached and grasped her by the shoulders.

"You're not about to faint on me are you, Jessie?" he asked with concern as he led her to the closest chair.

Jessie sat down in the chair and then to her great surprise, bent her head into her hands with her elbows resting on her knees and wept.

All of her siblings stopped and stared at their sister with deep concern. They had never seen Jessie this way and it confused them.

Finally, Ryler made his way to his big sister and placed his chubby hand on her arm as he crooned, "It'll be awright, Jessie. Daddy's home now."

Lifting her head, Jessie looked affectionately at her little brother with his head of blond curls.

"I know, Ryler. That is why I am crying." Jessie looked at her father at this point and decided an explanation was in order.

"Mama made me promise on the day she died that I would keep all of us children together. She knew we would be separated into foster homes once she was gone so she told me to flee if necessary. That is what we had to do and though it has been very difficult, I have kept my word to her."

McKaine stared lovingly at her and then knelt down and hugged his eldest daughter. "Jessie, I am so very proud of you. I don't know what I would have done if I had returned to find all of you separated into so many homes. Thank you . . . . . for me and your mother."

Hugging her father every so tightly, Jessie wept it out and then pulled back. "But had we not better be getting ready and go rescue Grandpa?"

"Yeah! Let's go get Grandpa!" All the little ones and Josh shouted in unison.

Sarah moved quickly at this point, clapping her hands to gain the attention of her younger siblings. She began scrubbing little faces and grubby hands. Jessie arose and began combing each child's hair as the older boys got themselves ready and fetched coats.

Mr. McKaine, sat down on the couch and observed this well-organized effort by his children to speed up the process. Tears came to his eyes as he thought about all he had missed in the past few years. Drying them at length, however, he considered the joys still to come in the future. Right now, however, they just needed to make every effort to get his father-in-law released as quickly as possible.

The girls freshened themselves up as Josh outfitted the little ones to go out into the cold. Micah called Wolf and made for the barn to provide hay for the burro and goats and close them in for the night. Then the girls and their father donned their own coats and grabbing some biscuits and water for the trip down the mountain, ushered the little ones outside.

Micah joined them and patting Wolf on the head instructed him to take care of everything while they were gone.

Wolf looked up with his wise eyes and watched as his family disappeared behind the waterfall and through the big wooden door.

The children were chattering excitedly as they made their way through the tunnel. They had not been out of the enclosure of the cabin and its grounds in a very long time.

Exiting from the cave at length, Jessie saw Sarah take a deep breath. It had to feel strange to her as she, in particular, had been cabin-bound for so long now.

The twins suddenly spied Thunder and immediately wanted to ride him down. Their father laughed as he realized this had been a dream of his little boys for some time now.

"I'll tell you what, all of you little ones will be allowed to ride one at a time as we travel down. The trail is too dangerous and this stallion is too spirited for more than that."

"You must obey the rules, too. The first one who spooks the horse or yells will be handed down and not allowed to ride again on this trip. Have I made myself clear?"

Four little heads nodded seriously and then grinned broadly at the prospect of riding Thunder.

"Since the first part of the trail is the steepest and hardest to navigate, we will start with Annie. Micah, if you will hand her up to me, she can sit right in front and hold on to the saddle horn."

Annie's little face was wreathed in smiles as she sat surrounded by her father's arms. She dutifully held on tightly to the horn with both chubby little hands and giggled softly as they began their journey.

Thunder led the way with Jessie and Sarah following at a safe distance. The twins marched directly behind them and then Josh. Katy had hung back in order to walk with Micah who was bringing up the rear and keeping a close watch on his family.

With the exception of Josh and Micah, the children had not been off of this mountain since the day of their arrival here. How excited they were to be descending the trail once again!

Jessie thought about what all this meant and could hardly wrap her mind around the changes which were quickly coming their way. The load had been completely lifted from her shoulders. She had kept her word. She had struggled to keep them all together but now, all of a sudden, her father had that responsibility and she could finally relax completely.

What a wonderful day and such a heady feeling! How she had longed for this and now here it was and she was walking in this enormous blessing with her father leading the way!

When they arrived at Shelter Rock, their father stopped and handed Annie down to Jessie. They all took a break and the children talked incessantly. No worries about keeping them quiet anymore. Their exuberance knew no bounds.

Soon it was time to continue on and since Ryler was the second youngest, though by only minutes, he was allowed to ride next. It was hard for him to rein in his excitement, but his father was firm about not spooking the horse so he obeyed implicitly.

Jessie carried Annie for a while and then Micah put her on his shoulders and carried her there. She was almost as excited about riding on her brother's shoulders as she had been about riding a horse!

Roughly half-way down, their father stopped again for another rest and handed Ryler down. The little boy ran around like an Indian as he could finally release his pent-up energy.

Watching his son with great affection, Mr. McKaine finally spoke up, "You had better save some of that energy, Ryler. We still have a long way to go."

Soon they were underway again. Jessie was secretly glad as the air was decidedly colder now and walking helped keep them warmer. She wrapped Annie in a blanket from her backpack and held her close as the little one shivered. Micah had also wrapped Katy in a blanket as she was shivering uncontrollably.

Sarah, too, had donned a blanket around her shoulders. Staying inside so much, she was unaccustomed to the colder temperature. She was also not used to the strenuous exercise and it was growing a little long for her.

Jessie kept a close watch on her sisters, but could only see joy written on each precious face. They truly did not mind the discomfort as long as they could be with their dad.

Tyler was enjoying his ride on Thunder immensely. He was also getting to know his father better and was asking a lot of boyish questions.

At one point, Jessie saw her father throw his head back as he laughed quietly at something Tyler had said.

In a way, Jessie wished this trip down the mountain could last forever. For a long time they had waited and prayed for just this very thing. Their father was home and leading his family out of their seclusion! What a wonderful time they were having!

It would not be long before Grandpa would be released from jail. It would not be long before Jessie could see Raine freely. Jessie's heart was near to bursting again with her great happiness!

Coming back to earth, Jessie realized that her father was stopping again. He hopped down and tied Thunder to a tree beside the trail. Then he lifted Tyler down. Running immediately to his twin brother, Tyler began telling of his adventure riding "the big horse."

Mr. McKaine stretched his arms and legs and then reached for a very sleepy Annie. He held her close against his chest, wrapping the blanket more snuggly about her.

"It won't be long kids until we reach the Roberts farm. I feel certain they will let you warm up there. I will make some phone calls and see how far we can get towards getting your grandpa released today. If not today, then certainly tomorrow the authorities should release him."

"Yeah!" the children yelled which caused Thunder to start.

Their father walked back over to the big stallion and stroked and soothed him. Then he returned to his children.

"It is time for Katy to ride. And if you don't mind Katy, I think we should take Annie, too. It looks like she will sleep the rest of the way. That will give your brothers and sister a break from carrying her."

Little Katy nodded her head in her most mature fashion as she shivered uncontrollably, "She should ride Daddy. Maybe she will be warmer that way."

Her dad smiled lovingly at her, "And, maybe you will be too, sweetie."

Jessie and Micah worked to strap Annie to their father's chest. When she was secure, Mr. McKaine climbed upon Thunder's back and situated Katy in front of him as Micah handed her up. They wrapped a blanket securely around her and Thunder headed out to carry his load back to the farm.

The rest of the children were still so excited that they were not showing any sign of fatigue yet. The exception was Sarah. She was completely wrapped in the blanket she had donned. The twins did not even seem to notice the cold, however.

The rest of the trip down the mountain went without incident. In Jessie's heart and mind this very special family time ended all too soon.

She could not be sad about that, however, as she knew she would be seeing Raine shortly. Her heart literally raced at the thought!

Jessie noted that the car had returned as they approached the farmhouse. Her father instructed her to knock on the door and ask if the children could warm up there while he took Thunder to the barn to get his saddle off and care for him.

Before she could knock, however, the kitchen door opened and Grandma Nattie greeted them all, "Come in. Come in out of this cold!" she admonished.

Jessie stepped inside and greeted Uncle Charlie, who was leaning against the kitchen counter. She reached behind her and ushered in the twins and then Katy who was holding hands with Sarah.

As she glanced back out, she saw Micah untying Annie from his father and Josh holding Thunder's reins.

Jessie's siblings stood smiling at Grandma Nattie who was leaning down introducing herself. The twins very happily met her and then dashed to the counter to hug their Uncle Charlie.

Grandma Nattie then held her arms out to hug Katy who responded to this grandmotherly nature instinctively.

"What lovely hair on such a lovely child!" Grandma exclaimed as Katie smiled at her while shyly whispering her thanks.

Rising, once again, Grandma beheld Sarah who smiled her beautiful smile and then to everyone's surprise, Grandma signed, "You are beautiful!"

Sarah blushed deeply and signed back, "Thank you."

Jessie hearing her brothers on the porch, turned and opened the door to let them in. Holding a sleepy Annie, Micah entered followed by Josh.

"Oh, my!" Grandma exclaimed when she saw Annie, "Would you let Grandma Nattie hold you," she asked, her face wreathed with smiles.

Annie held out her chubby little arms to Grandma and smiled demurely. Taking her in her arms, Grandma spoke to Micah and Josh over Annie's curly head. "You boys come on in and get yourselves warm. Then wash up. We are going to be eating in two shakes of a sheep's tail. Raine said you were coming so I have been cooking all afternoon and it is ready. If you girls will set the table, I will sit here in the rocker with Annie."

The rest of the children greeted their uncle and then headed to the bathroom before washing up. It had been a long trip down after all.

Jessie, Sarah and Katy were in the midst of setting the table when their father walked in. Uncle Charlie hobbled across the room at sight of him and the two shook hands affectionately.

"It appears we have a few things in common," Uncle Charlie spoke first, "We have both apparently been missing for approximately the same length of time. Neither one by our own choice, I understand."

"It certainly wasn't my choice to be away from my family this long," Mr. McKaine admitted.

"Well, it was my choice in a way," Uncle Charlie confessed, "but I know better now."

Jessie's father glanced at the girls setting the table and raised his brows, "Girls we don't want to impose on the Robert's hospitality . . ."

"Nonsense!" Nattie called out from the rocking chair.

"I have been cooking all afternoon expecting you. You have to be hungry after such a long walk!" she exclaimed.

"Well, if you insist, I won't argue with you," Mr. McKaine responded as he crossed the floor to introduce himself.

"Here, take this sweet little daughter of yours and I will go get the food on the table."

So saying, Nattie took charge of her kitchen and the taste buds of the whole family were watering at sight of the feast that she had produced.

Jessie noticed that their Uncle Charlie had apparently gained a few pounds since staying with Grandma Nattie and Raine. She smiled silently in approval.

As soon as Raine arrived in the kitchen he was enlisted to fetch extra chairs. Micah and Josh volunteered to help him and soon all was in readiness with seating for everyone at their large dining room table.

The children were all ravenous after their long hike and being in the cold. Grandma Nattie was prepared, however, and what was left over could have fed another crew.

In the course of the dinner conversation, Uncle Charlie asked gently if his nephew-in-law had been captured while serving in Vietnam.

The children's father looked around the table at his family and new friends and taking a deep breath while carefully choosing his words, replied. "Within a few weeks after arriving in Nam, I became a POW. I remained in that state until just recently. The fact that I am here today is nothing short of a miracle. I understand that I have been constantly bathed in the prayers of my family and friends. God, Himself, freed me and if I live to be a hundred I can never thank Him enough."

"Well, we both have a lot of thanking to be done, I'm reckoning," Uncle Charlie responded then fell silent.

Nattie immediately grabbed the platter of fried chicken and passed it around again, distracting the children and returning the conversation to celebrating the presence of these two "lost, but now found" men.

Finally, when everyone's hunger was satisfied, Mr. McKaine gathered up his children, loaded them into his rental car and headed down the road to fetch Grandpa. Having been incarcerated for so long himself, he understood that even a few minutes would make a huge difference to his father-in-law.

He expected that his children would probably sleep most of the way down, but to his amazement, they all remained awake. Annie was the surprise to everyone, until they realized that she had never seen headlights, streetlights or just lights going by at night in general. Having been a baby when they arrived on the mountain, she, of course, had no memory of anything. She was mesmerized by the car and how fast they were going. Literally everything was new to her. Actually, she had never seen another human being outside of her siblings and Grandpa, until Raine and Uncle Charlie had appeared at their door.

This was indeed the biggest day of her not quite three years. Her little eyes were huge with the wonder of it all. The other children tried to explain all of these new things to her, but then everything was new to Annie!

Mr. McKaine drank in the happy chattering of his children and felt as if he should pinch himself to make sure it was all real. He had endured so much in the past years, but that was all over now and he was blessedly reunited with his children once again. He intended to make the most of each day now. There was certainly a lot to iron out, but he knew if he just asked God to guide him, he would be making the wisest of decisions.

Almost before they knew it, they had arrived at the jail where Grandpa was being kept. Swinging Annie upon his hip, he admonished the others to keep up and they all marched inside.

CHAPTER TWENTY-NINE

GRANDPA HAD GONE to bed early, but he was not asleep. He had been praising God for the safe return of his son-in-law. He knew the man was deeply grieved about the loss of his wife, Grandpa's only daughter, but he also knew that grief would be tempered by the joy of being reunited with his children. He prayed fervently for all of his family, as was his custom. He recognized that his ordeal would soon be over and he was excited about the prospect of being reunited with his grandchildren and only brother, as well as his recently returned son-in-law.

So lost was he in his thoughts and depth of prayer that it startled him when he heard the key inserted into the lock on his cell door. Whatever was going on? The doors were never unlocked at this hour of the night!

Then he heard the roughened voice of the guard, "Get on up, McAlister! The judge wants to see you."

"The judge!" Grandpa exclaimed in his confusion.

"That's right. Don't keep him waiting," the guard replied.

Grandpa quickly donned his clothes and ran callused fingers through his gray hair. He hurried down the corridor with the guard at his side. Whatever could be going on at this hour?

The judge looked irritable when finally, Grandpa was ushered into his presence.

"Kevin McAlister?"

"Yes, sir," Grandpa responded to the simple question.

"Some new light has been shed on your case. It would appear you are not guilty of kidnapping after all. As a matter of fact, someone has confessed to taking YOU off in the middle of the night. There is still the little matter of your withholding evidence from the State in this case, but due to extenuating circumstances, that charge against you has been dropped."

"It has been brought to my attention that your checking and savings accounts have been fraudulently accessed. Law officers are on the way as I speak to bring in your adopted son for questioning. I will expect you to stay in the area for a few days until we can ascertain the veracity of these charges. Otherwise you are free to go."

Grandpa simply stood in astonishment as the words sunk in. He was still staring at the judge with tears dropping off his chin when he saw the judge give a sign to the guard at the door. As the door opened, his grandchildren rushed inside uttering squeals of joy at sight of their grandpa.

What ensued was more tears as he was hugged and hugged again by the children with everyone wanting to talk at once.

Finally, the judge stood to his feet. With a loud "Ahem" he gained everyone's attention.

"I hate to interrupt this happy occasion, but I must return to bed and get at least a few hours' sleep before I return for my early cases tomorrow. It is apparent to me, however, that the State has misjudged you, Mr. McAlister. All I see is great love and trust in this room," his voice breaking at this point the judge turned to go.

After a brief pause, Ryler called out, "Thank you, Mr. Judge," and then everyone spoke at once thanking the judge for coming out at such an hour and what it meant to them.

The judge departed with a smile playing at the corner of his mouth. The family watched him go and were then ushered to the outer door by the guard. Grandpa turned at the last minute and shook hands with this man who had been kind to him during his incarceration. He was instructed to wait just a moment as someone had been sent to retrieve his personal effects.

Shortly thereafter, stepping out into the cold of the evening, Grandpa paused and took a deep breath of the fresh air. Was this really happening? Was he free at last?

He did not have to wonder long, however, as the children surrounded him, grabbed both hands and led him to the waiting car.

It was a tight squeeze in the back seat for Micah, Sarah and the younger ones but they did not have far to go. Also, it did not take long for the older children to realize that their father was taking them home - to their old house.

It was apparent to Micah that Sarah was becoming stressed by this fact so he leaned over and whispered, "Sarah, the judge said Sean was being picked up and besides Dad will take care of us now. Just relax, Okay?"

Sarah looked back at her brother with eyes that were still as big as saucers. She smiled a tremulous smile and then grabbed his arm and gave it an affectionate squeeze of thanks.

Driving into their old driveway felt strange, indeed, to Jessie. A quick look told everyone that Sean had let the house and grounds go down. There was neglect and disrepair everywhere.

The men exited the car first and approached the darkened house. After knocking repeatedly, they decided that Sean, indeed, was not there. Jessie's father extracted his key and opened the kitchen door. He and Grandpa entered and made a thorough search of each room. Finally, they decided it was too dirty to bring the children into at this hour.

They returned to the car and left to find motel rooms for the night. Poor Annie had tried with great determination to stay awake, but had finally succumbed to her heavy lids and lay sound asleep in Jessie's arms.

The boys and their father and grandfather carried the backpacks into the rooms they had rented for the night and everyone was soon settled for bed.

Micah and Josh were to room with their father and grandfather and the girls had all of the little ones in their room.

Josh drifted off as soon as his head hit the pillow but the men and Micah stayed awake far into the night planning the best course for the family to take.

They finally decided that they would call the next day and determine what had happened with Sean. Making sure that he was behind bars, they would return to their old house, clean it up and stay there until things were settled and Grandpa was truly at liberty to leave.

Grandpa felt that, in light of all that had happened here, it would be best to move the children back to the mountains soon after that. Jessie would be marrying and living there on Raine's farm and he believed keeping everyone fairly close together would be better for the whole family.

The children's father agreed but wanted to allow them the opportunity to voice their opinion in the matter since they had been through so much.

Micah was strangely quiet during this time. His father noted this and planned to talk to him one on one later and find out just what he was thinking.

The men finally said their "goodnight's" and turned in to get some much needed sleep.

CHAPTER THIRTY

MR. MCKAINE TOOK his family to breakfast the next morning and after ordering, left to make his phone call about Sean. The twins could not remember ever having eaten out before. Of course, Annie had never eaten out so everything was so different to her. They were all wide-eyed with wonder at their new-found freedom.

Grandpa was relishing each moment with his precious family. His happiness knew no bounds. The only point of sadness was his feeling that he had failed with Sean. He put it from his mind, however, and vowed to continue to pray for this man he had raised. He firmly believed that Sean had to come to the end of himself before he would turn to God and that is what he prayed.

The younger children could not believe they could order whatever they wanted. They were all accustomed to eating the same meals. As it turned out, most of them ordered pancakes anyway, however.

Their father soon returned with the news that they were at liberty now to return to their former home. They would spend the day cleaning and plan to stay there starting tonight.

Micah and Jessie exchanged looks and then glanced Sarah's way. She had gone a little pale.

It was not possible to worry about anything on this special day, however. They were all together at last! Their prayers had been answered! All they knew to do was be grateful for this tremendous blessing and they were that!

Soon breakfast was over and the short trip to their old home was behind them.

The younger children piled out of the car and ran through the leaves in the yard like wild Indians. Their father laughed out loud at their antics and then commissioned Josh to find some rakes, if there were still any there, and begin raking the yard with the little ones.

Jessie grabbed Sarah's hand as their father unlocked the kitchen door and held on tightly as they entered.

"Let's see what we will need in the way of cleansers and tools and then Sarah and I will make a trip to the store and lay in some supplies and groceries," their father stated as he glanced around at the mess that used to be his home.

Jessie gave a quick glance her father's way and then understood. He was immediately giving Sarah a new task away from the home. He was already applying wisdom in his leadership of his family. Her heart gave a huge leap of gratitude and relief.

While Sarah and her father surveyed the kitchen for their needs, Jessie and Micah checked out the pantry and bathroom storage. The cupboards were pretty bare. They would need most everything.

Sarah and her father left almost immediately and Jessie, Micah and Grandpa began the task of cleaning out the debris and taking the mattresses outside to air out.

As they drove to the store, Mr. McKaine addressed the issues in Sarah's heart.

"My darling, Sarah. I want you to understand that your father is home now and fully in charge. You are under my protection and care. I do not intend to allow anything to harm you. You can relax and go back to our old house without fear. Do you understand what I am saying?" he asked gently.

Sarah turned her beautiful big eyes upon her father. He noted they were rimmed with tears and his heart broke for her.

Then she scooted over close on the front seat and leaned her head on her father's shoulder. He heard her take a deep, shuddering breath and when she looked his way again, the fear had left her eyes.

"Now that is settled, I want you to know that you will be buying our groceries in the future. Jessie will be married soon and I am going to need to rely on your management skills to run this household. I understand that you are a natural, though you have not been in a store for a long time. Today is just the beginning of weekly shopping trips for you. Are you all right with this?" he asked.

Sarah's eyes grew wide as she thought on this. She had been on the mountain in seclusion for so long. Could she go back into the public and function there again?

She did not immediately answer her father. He glanced her way several times and finally decided he might have pushed her too hard. She was fragile after all, as everyone knew.

"If you are not ready yet for this responsibility, we can take it a little at a time," her father pursued gently.

Still she did not answer and by now Mr. McKaine was becoming a little alarmed. Maybe he was on the wrong track.

Finally, Sarah turned and signed, "I don't know, Dad."

"Fair enough," her father responded, "We'll just move at your pace, okay?"

Sarah smiled uncertainly and signed, "Okay" as they pulled into the grocery store parking lot.

Exiting the vehicle, Mr. McKaine noticed that his daughter remained in her place. He took a deep breath and went around, opening the passenger door. Sarah climbed out and stood beside him, looking around the parking lot.

He gently grasped her hand and when she looked up at him he smiled back at her with a confidence he did not feel.

As they entered the store, he noted that Sarah was getting her share of stares. This seemed to make her very uncomfortable, however.

Leaning down he whispered in her ear, "Sarah, there is not a young man in this store looking your way who is not thinking how very beautiful you are!"

Sarah turned a very attractive pink as she glanced around her and saw the admiration in the eyes of everyone looking her way. After all, none of them knew she could not speak. Maybe her dad was right, though she did not know how that could be.

As her father pushed the cart, Sarah locked her arm in his until she realized that he was wanting her to make the selections. When she did not comply, he picked up a very expensive item and placed it in the cart. Sarah looked at her father with dismay and then her economical nature kicked in. She removed the item from the cart and placed it back on the shelf. Then she carefully made her selection.

Her father turned his head and smiled. It was working. She just needed to be jump-started.

More young men stopped in their tracks to gaze on Sarah's beauty, but she was oblivious to them now. She was shopping for her family and they needed their money to stretch as far as it would go. She was focused on their needs and joy of cooking for them later.

By the time the bag boys had fallen all over themselves in order to be able to bag groceries for such an uncommon beauty, father and daughter had purchased enough groceries and supplies to last them for a few days.

Arriving back home, they discovered the yard was littered with debris and mattresses airing out. The little ones were playing in the leaves that had been raked into piles. Sarah laughed silently at their antics.

Micah and Josh ran to help their father with his purchases as Sarah made her way to the kitchen to begin making their lunch.

Jessie had finished scrubbing out the refrigerator and was working on the cabinets. The kitchen already looked and smelled so much better!

Glancing Sarah's way, Jessie noted the pink flush on her cheeks and decided she would want to tell her all about her shopping experience later when they had a break.

Helping Sarah put the grocery items away, Jessie noted two large loafs of bread. They had not had store-bought bread in almost three years. Things were certainly going to be different now!

CHAPTER THIRTY-ONE

SARAH WAS IN her element in the kitchen and their first meal back in their old house went very well. Everyone was starved after all of their work but soon they were filled and ready to start again.

Jessie thought back to their first meal in the cabin and how everyone had pitched in and worked so hard. Tears came into her eyes with the memory and she looked around on her family with pride.

Some of the walls were so stained now that it became evident that their best scrubbing efforts would not fix the problem. Their dad and Grandpa discussed the need for painting but it would have to be done at a later date. The true need now was to get the bedrooms ready for their first night.

The children's father elected to clean the master bedroom and Jessie was glad of this for everyone's sake. So many of the things they had treasured had been sold by Sean and that proved to be difficult. Going back to the room which so many of the treasures had graced would have been a hard thing for the children. As it was, their father would be assaulted with memories, but maybe it would be more healing for him, Jessie surmised. Of course, she would be praying for him and right now that was what he needed the most.

Jessie reminded herself as she had done so long ago that the real treasures were busy cleaning the house and grounds right now. Peace flowed once again into her heart as she thought on this.

After a time, Sarah left off cleaning and began their evening meal. She was excited about having such a selection of food items from which to choose. She would make a very special meal for her family's first night in their home again.

Later, as everyone sat around the dining room table, the children's father blessed their food. "Lord, we cannot thank you enough for how you have protected us and provided for all of our needs. We pray you would give us wisdom now as we move into the future. Guide us each step of the way and keep us healthy and strong for all that we must do. We are grateful for the bounty on our table and pray that you would bless it and the loving hands that prepared it. In your precious Son's name, amen."

There were tears in the eyes of the children and Grandpa as they passed the bowls of food. How very wonderful for all to be together again!

Later after their baths, no one had any difficulty falling to sleep. Their hard labors had earned them that.

The cleaning went on for the rest of the week and then the painting. They all rejoiced at the restoration of their old home. One evening, however, after everyone had finished for the night, Annie, nestled in her father's arms began to cry softly.

Her father, peering at her with consternation asked, "Annie, dearest, why are you crying? Do you not feel well?"

Annie ducked her head and did not answer.

"Please, Annie. You can tell your father. What is wrong?" her dad persisted.

Looking up into his eyes, Annie, with chin quivering, answered him, "I miss Wolf and . . . and the tabin."

Hugging her close, her dad looked around the living room at his children who were either occupying chairs or sprawled on the floor. "Does anyone else feel this way?"

Most of the children looked away and Jessie and Sarah dropped their eyes. No one answered, however.

"I take it by your silence that you all feel this way. Is that true?"

Finally, it was Sarah who signed the answer, "We don't belong here anymore, Dad. We want to go home."

Looking around the room at each of his children, their father simply stated, "I don't belong here either. I want to start a new life with my family on Charlie's mountain."

The children all looked at him incredulously. Could it be they were going home? Then all eyes fastened on Grandpa as a huge grin split his face.

"I think we have our answer, Son." Grandpa looked lovingly at Annie, "Out of the mouth of babes . . ."

CHAPTER THIRTY-TWO

THERE HAD BEEN such release with the acknowledgement that they all wanted to go home. Their old home just held too many sad memories and what Sean had done to it was difficult to take. At least, with all the repairs, cleaning and painting it could be sold now.

Finding Grandpa outside alone while he pruned dead limbs, the children's father thought it was the perfect time to approach him. "Grandpa, do you think Charlie would consider selling me his mountain?"

Looking at the dead grasses under the tree, he hesitated for a moment before answering. "You know, Charlie bought that mountain for Amy before we were even married. So it has been a sore spot between us. You would just have to pray about how to approach the matter. It would certainly be an answer for him, however. I do not think he will ever recover enough to live there on his own. Selling it would be the best thing for him."

"That is what I was thinking. The children consider that home and I would really hate to disappoint them if he won't sell it to me. Of course, he might rent it to us, but I have years of back pay coming to me and the sell of this house should put me in a good position to buy it."

"I will be praying for you, Son," Grandpa responded as he watched the children playing in the far side of the yard.

"You are welcome to continue living with us. We could add another room to the cabin."

Grandpa quickly interrupted him, "Natalie offered me quarters in her bunkhouse and I believe I will take her up on it. She also offered the same arrangement to Charlie. He would be wise to do the same thing. Jessie's young man has big plans for their future and I think I will fit into those plans rather nicely. Of course, as long as I am still able, I will make trips up the mountain to visit. And, I am sure the kids will be visiting the farm on a regular basis. If Charlie will just sell, I believe everything will fall in place."

Gazing up into the tree to check for any more dead branches, Grandpa left his son-in-law to consider his words.

"I will help you with the rest of these limbs, then I think I will go into town and talk to a realtor," the children's father announced as he, too, gazed into the tree.

"I would appreciate the help and if you don't mind I think I will clean up and go into town with you. I want to finish settling my affairs, here."

Both men lent their muscles to the job and finished just before lunch. The house and grounds were now pretty much completed and should show well to a prospective buyer.

CHAPTER THIRTY-THREE

LISTING THE HOUSE for a price that was fair and should encourage offers, the children's father finalized his business and the preparations for the trip back to the mountains began in earnest.

The siblings were beside themselves with excitement, especially Jessie who could not wait to see Raine. Renting a small moving trailer, they packed the furnishings they were taking and their suitcases. Grandpa, Micah and Josh elected to ride back on a bus in order to allow room for everyone in the car. Never having ridden in a bus before Josh was really looking forward to the adventure. My . . . how life had changed!

Hours later the car, towing the trailer, pulled into Nattie and Raine's farm. Nattie emerged from the farmhouse with her face wreathed in a welcoming smile. The twins ran to her as if she had been their grandmother. Katie and Sarah, holding hands, approached her more sedately.

Jessie and her father, who was holding a just awakening Annie, waited their turn to greet Jessie's future mother-in-law.

As Jessie was enveloped in a big hug, Nattie whispered in her ear, "He is in the barn with the colt. Hurry on out and see him!"

Giving Nattie a grateful smile, Jessie turned and ran to the barn.

"You must be hungry after your trip. Go get washed up and I will put everything on the table," Nattie began only to be interrupted by the children's father.

"Oh, no. We did not come for a meal," Mr. McKaine began.

"Nonsense, the food is already prepared. You just need to sit down and eat it. Now if someone will just go fetch Charlie. He is in the bunkhouse."

The twins turned immediately to run to the bunkhouse. Their father handed Annie off into the waiting arms of Nattie and hurried to catch up with his rambunctious boys.

Raine looked up as Jessie quietly approached the stall. He stood to his feet and slowly made his departure from the skittish colt. His eyes, however, were devouring the woman he adored.

The hug he gave nearly took Jessie's breath away. In a split second, Jessie had a glimpse into her future and she knew she would experience great happiness with this man. After all, had not God brought them together. Of this Jessie had never had a doubt.

The family came back together in the kitchen where Sarah and Nattie worked like a well-ordered team. There was so much excitement at being together again. Nattie's heart overflowed with joy at the amount of love that filled her large kitchen.

"Katie tells me that Kevin and your older sons chose to ride back on the bus," Nattie began, addressing the children's father.

Nattie began, addressing the children's father.

"Yes. It would have been a little hard squeezing everyone into the car. Their bus should arrive in a couple of hours."

"Then we must go ahead and get this meal underway so you will have the time to reach the station before their arrival."

Soon, everyone was seated and Nattie requested that Mr. McKaine offer up their thanks.

"Father, we cannot begin to thank you enough for bringing us all safely back together. Your Hand has led us every step of the way, has healed Charlie, released Grandpa and given us wisdom for our decisions. Nattie and Raine have graciously accepted us into their midst and shared their bounty with us. It is You we praise, however, for we know that You have orchestrated all of our affairs. Thank you, Lord, for the feast that we are about to receive and strengthen us to do your will. In the name of your precious Son, Jesus, we pray."

Nattie, with tears flowing down her cheeks, reached to pass a bowl of mashed potatoes around. Even the children were hushed by their father's prayer as other bowls and platters were passed and the older ones helped to spoon such a delicious meal onto the plates of the little ones.

Jessie looked at Raine with gratitude in her eyes. She had known that Nattie kept a feast prepared and they would enjoy her labors when they reached the farm house. The others, however, had yet to learn this about Nattie.

Soon, everyone was filled to overflowing and it was time to leave to pick up the other family members.

Raine spoke up as Mr. McKaine rose to depart. "Listen, you have travelled quite a distance today and I will be glad to ride down to the station and pick up the others. Jessie could ride with me if she wanted."

Jessie longed to go with him, but quickly protested, "Oh, Raine, I need to stay and help clean up."

She was immediately interrupted by Nattie, "Jessie, I can take care of things here. You just go on with Raine now."

Making a shooing motion with her hands, Nattie finished, "Now scoot, you two!"

Grinning her gratitude, Jessie with Raine at her side, headed to the door.

"Actually, Charlie, this will give me some time to discuss something with you if you don't have any other plans right now." Mr. McKaine proposed.

"Only plans I have are to walk off some of this good cooking before Nattie makes me fat." Charlie frowned at Nattie but then chuckled good-naturedly.

"That will work for me, too, I think," Mr. McKaine responded.

The twins immediately wanted to go, but Nattie in her insight proposed showing them some of the toys Raine had when he was growing up. That deflected them and their dad and Uncle Charlie were able to depart with no difficulties.

The wind was brisk as Mr. McKaine and Uncle Charlie made their way down the dirt road to the bunkhouse.

Raising his eyes to the heavens as they walked along Uncle Charlie finally spoke, "My old bones tell me we have some winter weather coming. You best get these kids situated before it hits."

"That is actually what I was wanting to discuss with you," the children's father replied.

"Let's get inside and I'll stoke up the wood stove," Uncle Charlie hobbled up the one step and opened the door.

"Well, it is nice and warm in here. A lot more spacious than I thought it would be, too." Mr. McKaine commented with satisfaction as he surveyed the quarters.

"Look at all them quilts on the beds. Natalie made every one with her own hands. There'll be no getting cold in here, even if the fire should go out. But I'm sure that you saw that huge stack of wood we just passed on that there screened-in porch. It should last all winter. Easy gotten, too."

"I am glad to see you are so well fixed, Charlie. You certainly deserve it after all you have been through."

"Nattie insists on having me for every meal, too. She is a downright saint. Jessie couldn't have done any better for a mother-in-law."

"I would have to agree with you there," the children's father stated from his heart as he fingered the thick quilts on the beds. "These quilts aren't just thick and I'll bet warm, they are beautiful, too."

"Yeah. Nattie and her husband took good care of their help. This farm was a going concern when he was alive."

"So, you are planning on staying here right on?" Asked Mr. McKaine.

"In my present physical condition, there is no way I could ever go back to the cabin. Even when I am fully recovered, I don't think it would be wise at my age. I paid for my needs by traipsing all over Castleknob harvesting ginseng. I grew all my foodstuffs, raised chickens and hogs and got my milk from the goats. While I can still do most of those things, my ginseng hunting days are over. I would just be asking for trouble if I tried to do that again with a bum leg."

"Nattie and Raine have offered me these quarters and my meals. They would give it to me for nothing but I won't settle for that!" Uncle Charlie shook his head vehemently for emphasis.

"I told them I would pull my own weight here or nothing doing!"

"So, if that is settled do you have any future plans for Castleknob?" Mr. McKaine inquired.

Uncle Charlie looked up with a twinkle in his eye, "Well, I thought you and them kids might be wanting it. They certainly seem smitten with it."

The children's father smiled broadly, "They are indeed! They were so homesick for Castleknob they had an out and out celebration when I told them we would see what we could do about it!"

Uncle Charlie threw his head back and guffawed at that.

"I have some back pay and savings that Sean was unable to access so I just might be in a position to take it off your hands," Mr. McKaine began only to be interrupted by Uncle Charlie.

"I believe we can work things out." Uncle Charlie looked away as his eyes suddenly filled with tears. "You know I bought that mountain for the woman I believed was going to be my bride. She became my sister-in-law instead. Isn't it ironic that her own grandchildren have fallen in love with that very mountain and want to live their lives there? Nothing would please me more than seeing all of ya'll live your lives out there."

"You certainly have a good attitude about all of this," Mr. McKaine said softly.

"Listen, God has healed my hurt and my heart. He saved my life in that accident. He's provided a wonderful place for me to recover and live out my days surrounded by loving family and friends. What more could I ask?"

"I feel the same way you do, although my situation is different. It would be a blessed honor to buy Castleknob and begin again in such a beautiful place. Think about what you would have to have for it and let me know," the children's father turned to go, "By the way, are the back taxes resolved?"

"Nattie was going to take me to the courthouse this afternoon to take care of those. I have used up all my time with those folks. Tomorrow is my final day."

"I'll tell you what I'll do. I will pay them myself as part of my down payment until we can get the sale closed. Would that be all right with you?"

"Son, you have no idea what a blessing that would be! You're an answer to prayer. God always provides, doesn't He?"

Mr. McKaine approached the door and then turned around, "Yes, He does . . . He always does."

Uncle Charlie watched his nephew-in-law leave and then bowed his head to utter his thanks to the One who always provides. Then he laid his weary bones down upon his bed, covered himself with Natalie's quilt and took a much needed nap.

CHAPTER THIRTY-FOUR

RAINE REACHED TO hold Jessie's hand as they headed to the bus stop in Nattie's car. "You have no idea how much I have missed you!"

"Oh, I think I might have some idea," Jessie admitted with her special smile as she glanced sideways at him.

"Everyone is so excited about being back. Is there something I need to know?" Raine continued.

Jessie hesitated, "Raine, we simply don't fit in anymore in our old home and town. There are just too many memories there. Mostly good ones, but some bad ones and, of course, very sad ones. Annie finally did what none of the rest of us had the courage to do. She voiced that she wanted to go home."

"Annie?" Raine grinned at her, "Well, out of the mouth of babes."

"Yes, that broke the ice and we all admitted that we wanted to come back here to Castleknob. Even Dad and Grandpa wanted to do just that thing."

"That would be best for Uncle Charlie, too. He really does not need to live again on the mountain. He is not up to it. Of course, we want him to stay right on at the farm. He's welcome to live here the rest of his life and Grandma will take really good care of him. He has already gained weight and he seems to be fitting in very well. He wants to 'earn his keep' as he puts it, but Grandma tells him that will come later."

"Dad is wanting to buy Castleknob if Uncle Charlie will sell it to him. He was going to talk to him after we left. Dad already loves it there as much as the rest of us, I think. It will be a good place for him to recuperate, too."

"Whoa, wait a minute! You're living on the farm in a few weeks. Remember?"

"Oh, Raine . . . I would never forget that! I am looking so forward to being married to you and helping you make the farm into what you want it to be."

"Whew! You had me worried there for a moment!" Raine exclaimed as he drove into the bus station parking lot.

Jessie smiled lovingly at him as he opened the car door for her. Grasping her hand, Raine led her into the bus station and to the counter to check for arrivals.

They found the bus was only going to be a little late so the couple sat down to await the arrival of Jessie's brothers and Grandpa. They were enjoying just being together as they sat there. Suddenly, it occurred to Jessie that they would not have to be separated much anymore.

"Oh, Raine. It just hit me that this whole ordeal is finally over and we will not have to spend so much time apart."

Raine's grin was huge as he looked at her, "Now, I can start dating you in earnest. So, can I have the pleasure of a date tomorrow night? I will pick you up at your door, you know."

"Raine, that would be marvelous! I can hardly believe this is true. What time would you like me to be ready?"

"How about four o'clock? That would give us enough time to get down the mountain and to a restaurant at a decent hour."

"Four o'clock, it is. I can't tell you how much I will be looking forward to it."

The arrival of the bus drowned out any further comments. The two stood and looked happily for their loved ones. Suddenly, they heard Josh call out, "There is Jessie and Raine!"

Making their way through the few who disembarked, Jessie hugged her Grandpa first and then her brothers. Raine reached out his hand and grasped Grandpa's huge paw.

"I am so glad to see you, sir. It has been a very long time and I am not sure you remember me," Raine began.

"I surely do remember you," Grandpa exclaimed while still shaking Raine's hand. "You were quite a bit younger, however. You have certainly grown up to be a fine looking young man."

Raine reddened as Grandpa continued. "Son, I can never thank you enough for all of your efforts in taking care of my family while I was gone. I understand you also worked for my release. Words just cannot express my gratitude to you!"

Grandpa's voice had become husky with emotion and Raine discovered he could not reply.

Putting her arm around Raine, Jessie finally broke the silence "Both of you took such good care of all of my siblings and me. I am grateful beyond measure to you both."

Micah and Josh echoed the sentiments and soon tears were streaming down all of their faces. What a reunion! Jessie's heart was filled with love for all of them!

"You must be hungry as bears! Let's get your luggage and get you home so my grandma can feed you."

"We sent our luggage in the trailer with Dad," Micah informed Raine.

"Okay. Then let's be off. The car is parked out front."

The boys were full of details of their bus ride. It had been exciting for both of them. Grandpa smiled as they recounted their adventures which seemed to make the trip pass more quickly. They were back at the farm before they knew it.

Jessie noticed immediately that their dad's vehicle had been unhitched from the trailer and was gone.

Soon, the boys and Grandpa were sitting down to their part of the feast. Grandma had fried up some more chicken while the others had been gone. She was seeing to it, as usual, that everyone had their fill.

"Kevin, it is so good to have you back where you need to be - with your family. God truly answered our prayers!" Grandma affirmed.

"You and Raine and the children's father had your parts. I am eternally grateful for all you did, but you are right. God orchestrated it all," Grandpa eyes filled once more with tears as he acknowledged this.

"We will talk more on that later, but right now you need to be able to eat," Grandma asserted.

"Nattie, your cooking is as excellent as I remember!" Grandpa exclaimed.

"It's just country cooking, as you well know. You won't leave my table hungry, however. That was one of the things Caleb insisted on when we married. We were always one hundred percent in agreement on that point," Nattie replied with a far-away look in her eyes.

"Caleb was a good man. He was always hospitable, fair and honest in his dealings. Everyone in these parts knew him for that."

"He was a good man and I will always miss him, however, God is blessing me with a new family now and I could not be happier," Nattie responded with a smile, though tears rimmed her eyes.

"Speaking of family, is Charlie around today?" Grandpa asked with a little concern.

"Oh, my, yes! He was here to see everyone when they arrived, but he still needs to take a nap every afternoon. I'm sure that is where he is. But he is coming right along in his recovery. Chomping at the bit to help out around here. It has been hard to hold him back!"

"Of course, with Raine's plans, there will be plenty for everyone to do. We could use your skills, as well, Kevin. Jessie tells me you are quite the gardener."

"Well, that is something I dearly love to do. I would be honored to help you out. I am going to try to find a place to settle down now that the children's father is home. I will try to get one close by."

"Well, if you don't mind bunking with Charlie, we do have those quarters available. It is cozy and warm and comes with meals," Nattie offered.

"If you'll allow me to pay for it, I think that would work just fine," Grandpa began, only to be interrupted by Nattie.

"No, we won't accept pay for the bunkhouse and meals. That will be part of the pay package, depending upon how much work you want to do," Natalie responded.

"That is a most generous offer and one that I can hardly refuse. I think you have a deal," Grandpa responded with enthusiasm.

"Good! Charlie would have been very disappointed otherwise. He was counting on the two of you being bunkmates. Just unload all your things here and you can start living there today." Nattie turned as one of the twins wanted to ask her about Timo.

"I am being paged," she uttered happily as she arose from the table. But she turned back to smile at Grandpa, "I am glad that is settled. Welcome aboard!"

"Wow, Grandpa! You have a job and you have only just arrived!" Micah stated with admiration.

"That is just what I was needing, Micah. To get right to work," Grandpa responded with a look of satisfaction.

Hearing the crunch of gravel, Jessie and Raine exited the barn where they had been caring for the colt. Jessie, with trepidation, watched her father park the car.

"Since you are back, I am supposing all went well at the bus station," Jessie's father began as he exited the vehicle.

"Oh, yes. The boys and Grandpa are feasting at Grandma Nattie's table as we speak," Jessie responded.

"Well, good. That did not take long. Sometimes those buses can be quite a bit late."

"This one was almost on time, which was a blessing, as Grandpa seemed a little tired from riding," Jessie looked at her father questioningly. She was very curious about where he had been, but hesitant about asking.

Her father, however, saw the look and did not want to keep them in suspense any longer. "I have been to the courthouse, paid Uncle Charlie's back taxes and so we begin our down payment to purchase Castleknob," he announced proudly.

Jessie wanted to whoop in her happiness, but decided an engaged young lady should not behave in that manner. She could barely contain her joy at the news, however.

"Congratulations, Mr. McKaine!" Raine exulted. "God has certainly answered everyone's prayers!"

"And, in the nick of time, I might add," responded his father-in-law to be. "Tomorrow was the extension deadline."

Jessie's feet would hardly stay on the ground she was so happy. She grabbed her father in a big hug. It was SO good having him home again taking care of everything!

"Dad, I am so happy. Let's go and tell the others!" Out of the corner of her eye she detected a movement and turned to see her uncle making his way to the farm house.

"Here comes Uncle Charlie now. He will be so relieved to hear that is done!" Jessie exclaimed.

The trio waited for Uncle Charlie, who immediately saw the 'thumbs up' the children's father gave him and broke into a huge grin. The family entered into the warmth of the kitchen with elation showing on their faces.

Grandpa rose when he saw Charlie and gave him a big hug, "We are going to be bunkmates again, brother!" he stated happily.

Tears ran down Charlie's face as he looked at his brother. God had preserved his life, restored his memory, brought him back into a relationship with his only brother, given him a family in which to share, provided a warm, cozy place to live with excellent food and friends and enabled the sale of his property to the grandchildren of the only woman he had ever loved. His heart was so full of love and gratitude that he literally could not speak.

The children's father gave the two men some time and then said, "Everyone I have an announcement to make."

Nattie turned with a giggling Annie in her arms while the twins quieted down and looked at their father.

When everyone was giving their full attention, Mr. McKaine continued, "Uncle Charlie has graciously agreed to sell his beloved Castleknob . . ."

Some of the children groaned, but Nattie's eyes were twinkling as she looked at Grandpa.

"Wait before you become too downcast! He has agreed to sell Castleknob to me!"

The shouts of "hooray" drowned out further conversation for the moment. The younger children ran to their father and started hugging his legs. Natalie placed Annie on the floor and her chubby little legs ran as fast as they could to her father, who picked her up and held her close to his heart.

Uncle Charlie's smile almost broke his face as he observed this elation. The children really did love Castleknob. There could never be any doubt in his mind about that.

Finally, as the excitement began to abate, Ryler looked at Uncle Charlie earnestly, "What about Wolf? Where will he live?"

The children collectively held their breaths as they awaited this crucial answer. Uncle Charlie looked at each precious face and read the desire that was reflected there.

"Well, I reckon that Wolf, or King as I called him, has never known any other home than Castleknob. He might be homesick if we took him away from there. Just maybe Grandma Nattie and Raine wouldn't mind if he paid me a visit from time to time."

All the little children turned as one to see what Grandma Nattie would say. Sarah was actually still holding her breath.

"Family is always welcome on this farm. Now isn't Wolf or King," here Natalie looked affectionately at Charlie, "truly part of the family?"

At her answer, the children whooped their excitement again and Ryler spoke up once more, "Couldn't we change his name to King Wolf?"

Everyone laughed merrily and the children's father projected his voice to exclaim, "King Wolf it is!"

Nattie spoke up at this point to say, "Mr. McKaine I believe it is getting too late and there has been so much excitement today for your family to travel on up the mountain. I have plenty of beds for the children and if you men don't mind sleeping in the bunkhouse, I believe you should spend the night here."

Mr. McKaine looked at her with gratitude, "I was going to get motel rooms . . ."

"Oh, I wouldn't hear of such a thing! Girls come help me get the bedrooms ready and we will have one big slumber party!"

Jessie looked up and smiled her love at Raine, "You have a most special grandmother," she said softly.

"That I know very well," Raine responded.

Then he turned, "If any of you boys, or men would like to help me feed the livestock, I would enjoy the company. We can get the suitcases situated too."

Raine squeezed Jessie's hand as they each turned to go their separate ways.

He already was loving having such a huge family!

CHAPTER THIRTY-FIVE

THE NEXT TWO weeks passed more quickly than Jessie would every have imagined. She helped her family get situated once more on Castleknob and prepared for her wedding at the same time.

Grandma Nattie proved to be as excellent of a seamstress as she was a cook.

Jessie's mother's wedding dress was almost a perfect fit and became one with Grandma Nattie's few alterations. The little girls and Sarah received new dresses also made by her skilled hands with help from Sarah.

Trips to the store were made for undergarments, new shoes and suits for the boys, Grandpa and Uncle Charlie. Mr. McKaine's suit had to be altered because of all the weight he had lost but Grandma did not want to alter it severely because she knew other daughters were coming up and Mr. McKaine was sure to gain weight with the help of the mountain air and Sarah's good cooking.

There was so much to do that Jessie was unable to spend as much time with Raine as she had envisioned. However, they were able to have that one special date of which they had spoken.

Raine did indeed pick her up at the door of the cabin. Together they rode down the mountain on a beautiful clear and warmer day. Their breath still frosted the air but it was a day and night Jessie would never forget.

The restaurant where Raine had reserved their table was the fanciest one Jessie had ever seen. Her eyes were wide taking it all in. She clung to Raine's hand as they were led to their table and Raine ordered for her the specialty of the house.

Then Raine reached across the table and gently took Jessie's hand into his own large one, "Jessie, I have loved you so intensely for so long. It seemed it might never work out for us to be together at times. I just kept having faith, however, that God would arrange everything in His own good timing. I learned that faith from you and it has made me a better and stronger man."

Raine squeezed her hand and then withdrew his own and reached into his pocket. Withdrawing a small, ornate box, he held it in his trembling fingers. Slowly opening the lid, he reached in to withdraw a beautiful antique ring.

Jessie's eyes lit up at the sight of it. There was a beautiful fiery diamond in the center. Surrounding the diamond was two emeralds, two sapphires and two rubies. Jessie was so overwhelmed by its beauty that her hands flew to her face.

"Oh, Raine! This is exquisite!" She finally exclaimed.

"It belonged to my mother's grandmother. Her then fiancé had it made for her. He was a gemologist and actually found the emeralds, sapphires and rubies during his own digs in this area. Back then there was an emerald mine, which has since closed. As you may know this area is littered with sapphire and ruby mines. Finding quality like this, however, is rare today," Raine looked back up at Jessie with shining eyes.

Tears were streaming down her cheeks unchecked. She had never seen anything more beautiful.

Raine reached for Jessie's hand once again and slipped the ring upon her finger. "We are now officially engaged as well as enjoying our first date," he uttered softly.

CHAPTER THIRTY-SIX

THE DAY DAWNED bright and beautiful even though it was cold. Nattie had insisted that the entire McKaine family once again spend the night at the farm before the wedding. The girls were all in a flutter as they prepared their hair and donned their dresses. The little ones had never been to a wedding before so the rehearsal had been a real treat. They could not wait for this day's event!

The church looked lovely with its decorations of ivy and holly. Jessie had elected to keep things simple due to expenses, however, Natalie had convinced her that her wedding day should be fully celebrated. So with the help of some skilled ladies at church the decorations were tastefully done using materials from the area.

Jessie felt her father's hand gently grasp her elbow. She turned to look at him with such love coming from her eyes.

"You are beautiful!" he said softly. "You look so much like your mother. She would be very proud."

Her eyes shining, Jessie kept her composure. Then she looked down the aisle as Raine and Grandpa assumed their places. Choosing Grandpa as his best man had solved one of Jessie's dilemmas. She felt Grandpa should be included after all he had done for them but did not want to presume on Raine's rightful choice.

Her heart so full of love, Jessie could not get enough of how very handsome Raine looked and Grandpa, too.

As the wedding march began, Katie started down the aisle. She was so pretty in her new bridesmaid's dress. She curtsied sweetly when she came to the end of the aisle where the grandmother of the groom had just been seated. Nattie chuckled softly at this.

Sarah was stunning, as usual, as she walked with her natural grace to her position. The twins followed together carrying the pillow. They were grinning like two little Indians, relishing the attention.

Annie then preceded the bride with her basket of rose petals. There were 'oohs' and 'aahs' as she did her job to perfection.

Raine looked towards the back of the church at this point and his breath was literally taken away. He had never seen such a vision of loveliness and this beautiful creation coming ever so slowly down the aisle was to be his wife. Raine's eyes glowed with happiness.

Nattie, seeing Raine's look, could not have been happier herself. Long had she prayed for just such a woman as Jessie to bless his life. From the first moment she had set eyes on Raine in his little blue blanket, she had prayed for his future mate. God had answered her prayers in such a marvelous way! Her heart was full and overflowing with praise and love.

Grandpa had felt a clutch in his heart as he gazed upon Jessie. She looked so much like his beloved Amy. He glanced at Charlie and saw his face blanch. Jessie, of all the granddaughters looked the most like the woman they had both loved. Never had she looked more like her than today, however. Grandpa's eyes filled with tears at his memories. He gave Jessie a big smile, however. She certainly deserved this happiest of days after all she had endured for her family.

Arriving at the front of the church they both looked at the pastor as he asked, "Who gives this bride?"

Though there was a definite catch in his voice, her father spoke with clarity, "Her mother in heaven and I do."

Jessie, her eyes full of tears, turned and gave him a hug of gratitude. How like him to include her mother in this ceremony! As Jessie released her father, Raine stepped to her side. She looked up at him with such love. God had provided her with incredible blessings! How could she ever thank Him enough?

Raine looked down into Jessie's upturned face. So much love was there! How had he merited such a gift? God had blessed him beyond anything he could have ever hoped or imagined. He felt a fierce sense of responsibility for this woman. He intended to honor the vows that followed to the very best of his ability. His love for her was so immense that it would have to find its way out in expression each day that he lived. He was already thinking upon ways to bless her.

Jessie, as she uttered her "I do's" was committing each one in her heart to God above. Her face was "set like flint" to keep her words until her dying day. Her expression, however, was so relaxed and full of love.

At the time of exchanging of rings, the twins shared their responsibility with decorum. They each bowed to Jessie and then to Raine. Twitters were heard throughout the congregation of friends and family. Their gallantry, while heartfelt, was amusing, none-the-less.

Jessie and Raine turned to face everyone as the minister called out, "It is my great pleasure to present to you Mr. and Mrs. Raine Roberts." Then the two walked down the aisle and into their new life together - a life of faith, family and most of all, deep and abiding love.

EPILOGUE

TWO LITTLE BOYS rode past the farmhouse on matching ponies. They waved to their mother sitting on the porch shelling peas. Opening the screen door, Nattie emerged carrying a tray of ice drinks. Jessie looked up gratefully and reached over her extended belly to the cool drink that was offered.

"It won't be long now until we have another little one playing around the place," Nattie commented with a smile. "Are you sure you are not too hot sitting out here? It is cooler inside."

"What! And miss the twins riding their new ponies? Not for the world would I miss out on this!" Jessie exclaimed.

She looked across at the corral where Raine was tending to his herd of horses. They had raised so many through the years! Raine's endeavors had been successful beyond their own belief. With Nattie's skill their herb farm had grown considerably, as well. While their oldest son was following in his father's footsteps, their daughter loved working with plants. She was Natalie's right arm now.

Their twin boys, still riding past on their ponies were gifted with the farm animals and had many pets. She would deliver the new baby within the month. The way she was carrying this one, she was sure it was another girl.

Jessie looked up as she heard additional hoof beats. Twenty-five-year-old Sarah was approaching with her handsome husband of two years. Like Nattie, she rode her mount like a princess. She had matured into an incredible beauty!

As the two pulled up and tied their horses to the posts, Jessie could see the joy shining forth from her sister's face. Sarah had barely reached the porch before she was signing her good news. There would be another baby born in six months - her first.

Jessie struggled to raise her body from the rocking chair in order to give her sister a loving hug. How excited she was for her!

Sarah was full of family news, as well. They had heard from Micah. He would be home from veterinary school soon for the summer. He was hoping to establish a practice in Stekoah when he finished his schooling. He was planning to move in with Grandpa and Uncle Charlie in the bunkhouse and help around the farm if they would have him.

"Oh, of course!" Jessie exclaimed, "There is always work to be done around here and Raine would appreciate additional help. Grandpa and Charlie would love the company, too."

Sarah signed their father insisted on helping her husband with an addition to their cabin when he heard about the baby. They had left him at their cabin, which was at the base of Castleknob near the waterfall which formed the stream flowing by their old picnic rock.

She and her husband had come off the mountain in order to tell their good news and order building materials for the new addition to their cabin.

"Then you will come back by and have dinner with us before you start up the mountain again?" Nattie interjected.

Sarah smilingly looked at her husband. He grinned and exclaimed, "Miss one of Grandma Nattie's famous feasts? Never!"

Nattie called to the twins to ride over to the bunk house and let their great-uncle Charlie and great-grandpa know they would be having company for dinner. She then turned to the others, smiled with delight and headed to the kitchen to add more dishes to her fare.

The happy couple left and moments later the mailman drove up to the Roberts' box. Jessie greeted him and attempted to rise to get the mail.

"Just hold it right there, Miss Jessie. I'll bring the mail to you," the mailman, true to his word brought the stack to an appreciative Jessie.

"Oh, thank you! It is a little difficult to get up anymore," Jessie admitted.

Raine came over and the two men walked away to talk shop as the mailman waved his good-bye to Jessie.

Thumbing through the stack of mail, she discovered two important letters. Calling to her oldest son, she commissioned him to take the one to Grandpa. It was another letter from Sean and she knew her Grandpa would be anxious to get it.

Sean had brought so much sadness and fear into their lives at one point. Since Grandpa had won him to Christ, he had been a model prisoner, however. All of their years of praying for the errant family member had finally produced fruit. Grandpa now corresponded with him on a regular basis and visited him whenever possible.

Jessie turned back to the letter addressed to her. It was from Josh and she opened it expectantly. Josh, now twenty-one, was at med school. Her tender-hearted young brother wanted to dedicate his life to helping others. He was at the top of his class and had earned a major scholarship for his efforts. He, too, would be home for the summer staying with his dad and other siblings on Castleknob.

Thinking of those siblings now, Jessie sighed with satisfaction. Katy was another beauty at sixteen. It seemed all the boys in the valley were in love with her. She was so gay and bubbly, however, and entertained everyone she knew with kindness.

Ryler and Tyler had experienced many more adventures on Castleknob since their two-year-old quest to see more of "de tassel". They were strong and growing muscular now at the age of fourteen. They were a huge help to their father and the three of them had become the new ginseng harvesters on Castleknob. My, how things had changed, Jessie thought!

Her mind went back to her mother. It had been so painful to lose her, but they had kept their promise to her. The children had all remained together and were still so close. They had all participated in the raising of Annie, the one who had no recollection of any other mother than Sarah. She was going through a gangly stage at twelve, but would rival them all with her beauty one day soon.

As was her custom, Jessie's heart filled with praise for the wonderful God they all served, who had brought them through so many trials. She had learned to trust Him early on and Jessie wouldn't take anything for that trust now. She was confident that He would be with them in all of the trials that would come in the future. She could relax and live in great peace knowing this.

Hearing a whine, Jessie looked down into the upturned faces of Callie and King Wolf's offspring, Prince and

Princess. Prince tended to pal around with Uncle Charlie. They had a very special bond just as King had one time had with Charlie. Princess, on the other hand chose to stay close to Jessie and Nattie.

The other two descendants lived on Castleknob. One with her dad and siblings and the other was Sarah's constant companion, just as Wolf had been. Jessie stroked the silky heads and then arose with difficulty to do her part in preparing their meal.

Serving such a great God, her life filled with love and family, Jessie could not have been happier as she walked into the glorious future.

www.ingramcontent.com/pod-product-compliance
Lightning Source LLC
Chambersburg PA
CBHW032250150426
43195CB00008BA/387